Can I forget y

Also by Pamela Winfield

SENTIMENTAL JOURNEY:
the story of the G.I. brides
(in collaboration
with Brenda Hasty)

Pamela Winfield

CAN I FORGET YOU?

Coping with widowhood

Constable · London

First published in Great Britain 1987
by Constable and Company Limited
10 Orange Street, London WC2H 7EG

Set in Linotron Ehrhardt 11pt by
Rowland Phototypesetting Limited
Bury St Edmunds, Suffolk
Printed in Great Britain by
St Edmundsbury Press Limited
Bury St Edmunds, Suffolk

British Library CIP data
Winfield, Pamela
Can I forget you?: coping with widowhood
1. Widows
I. Title
306.8'8 HQ1058

ISBN 0 09 466390 4
ISBN 0 09 467890 1 Pbk

This book is dedicated to widows

'No one understands what it is like to be a widow until it happens to them. People may think they know how it will feel, but they can't, and you can't be cruel and tell any woman she will never really know until she lives it herself.'

The best thing a woman can do is scream – the sooner the better.

'Widowhood should not be the end of the world. It needs a certain readjustment of one's pattern of life, but it should not, by any means, be the end of life.'

Jehan Sadat

Contents

Acknowledgements

My thanks go to Helen Rosbottom, of the War Widows Association, who found me a widow from every recent war; Betty Arrieta in California, who supplied the American cuttings; Barbara Kidder in Oregon, who directed me to case histories on both sides of the Atlantic, and my library in South Audley Street, London W1, who constantly suggested books that would be useful. Then, there are all the friends who knew 'an interesting widow' and the ones I met along the way through the makings of this book. Several preferred to be anonymous.

Not everyone has been reported at the same length but I hope that all those who revealed their thoughts and feelings to me will find a few of their words within these pages. Some women have already had their stories chronicled by the media many times elsewhere. Therefore, their part in this book is concerned only with how they coped with widowhood.

Most important, I must mention Dahlia Witcher, who pulled me out of a crisis of confidence and sent me back to my desk. Without her, this book might well have been abandoned. Also, Elfreda Powell, who originally saw merit in the idea and ended up as my editor, putting the material into much better shape.

Pamela Winfield *November 1986*

Foreword

Many years ago, my first marriage ended in a horrifying car crash. I entered a new world, one for which I was, like any other young wife, totally unprepared. It was a strange and dangerous territory that no one can understand unless they have been there themselves. At first, sympathy had poured from what I anticipated was an un-turnoffable tap. There was, however, to be a turning-off point. Once they had done what they saw as their social duty, people became conspicuously absent. In my naïveté, I had expected that life would go on in reasonably the same way and that I would return to the world my husband and I had shared. It did not turn out that way.

I was the odd one out, though there were husbands who were willing to take pity on my 'lonely' state.

I poured my bitterness into an article which was rejected. Twenty-seven years ago, widowhood was not the subject-matter of conversation or magazines.

Eventually, like most widows, I got on with a new life in my own way. Later, I married again, and while I began to write on subjects that were acceptable, the circumstances of that early widowhood stayed with me and with them the idea of this book.

With the passing years, quite a few things have changed. Death is no longer the taboo subject that it was, and bereavement counselling is a growing service, but the attitude with which ordinary people view the widow's lot seems unchanged.

I hope that this book will make for a little more understanding of the widow's plight and her problems. I want to help her and explain to others how they might help her. Equally, I want to show new widows how other women can, and do, get on with their lives, and encourage them to do the same.

Introduction

Men and women marry together, but rarely die together. The change from being 'someone's wife' to 'the widow of . . .' is aptly described by one of them as 'like living through a bad dream, it's a catastrophe'. Bereavement is the most stressful of all situations – far worse than divorce.

Even when widowhood is expected because of a husband's terminal illness, it is still unexpected when it happens. One woman expressed her loss as like 'an amputation, and you have to get used to it, to live without': advice which is difficult to follow when some women cannot even say the words, 'My husband is dead'.

Even today, the large majority of women grow up with the idea that marriage is the most important goal in their life. For them, a husband symbolizes status; he is a living prop whom they do not foresee ever being without. Such a woman would come from the haven of her parents' home, straight into the shelter of marriage. There would now be a husband to take responsibility for her life, who could be relied on for everything, from paying the mortgage, to providing housekeeping and servicing the car. Without that man in her life, total panic can set in; she all too often sees her life as over. This woman can be recognized in the local High Street by her dazed look.

She is often accompanied by a briskly walking daughter trying to adapt her to shopping for one.

Not that the career woman who has juggled job, husband and children does any better. Widowhood leaves her just as devastated. So, in the first difficult months, these women, whose lives would ordinarily never overlap, find they share common ground.

There is no single face of widowhood. A widow is not necessarily an old lady heavily burdened by sorrow or a merry widow galloping into every spare bed. Such images inhibit, if they do not damage, her return to everyday life. Eighteen or eighty, the initial suffering is the same. So are most of the early steps reluctantly taken down widowhood's path.

The English word 'widow' is related to the French word *vide*, meaning empty, and many appear condemned to lead empty lives. Having been part of a pair, the half is no longer a whole. The widow finds she has become a spare, difficult to place. She represents what no wife wishes to be. In too many cases, her 'singleness' terminates established friendships. With such 'friends' she finds she is never fully accepted in her own right. It is as if she were blamed for upsetting the tidy pattern of pairs which makes up most of western life.

The resulting tactlessness can cause much pain; for example, there are some functions where tables might as well be labelled 'Widows only'. 'We like to mix', complained one lady who has too many times found herself in such a position. Hosts should bear this in mind.

Today's widow is distinguishable only by her tears, and after the initial grief and first rally of sympathy is over she is expected to keep that sorrow to herself. Perhaps, in earlier times, it was easier. The drama of widow's weeds and the fact that she retired from active life for a set mourning period gave her the chance she needed to adjust to her state. The new title, Widow Smith or Widow Jones, enabled her to view the world from behind a black veil. Nothing was expected of her until she was ready to set that veil aside.

After the First World War, East End widows adapted this practice to their style. They could be recognized by the custom of wearing their husband's pre-war work cap secured with an enormous hat-pin. These labels of widowhood worn with pride and dignity brought them a respect and consideration that now seems to be lacking.

Statistically, loss of a partner through death is more likely to happen to women than to men. At the last count, there were over 3 million widows to approximately 750,000 widowers in the United Kingdom. There are explanations for this. Traditionally, a husband is older. His work pattern may expose him to more stress and health risks. Most wives ignore the implications of these facts and give little thought to how they will manage without a husband. A wife may have a vague notion of insurance policies or savings. She may know a few details about his pension. But even the making of a will may have seemed distasteful and therefore have been postponed, since all such subjects seem to be pushed behind a wall marked 'Other People's Problems'.

Widowhood brings that wall crumbling down. Who will protect a wife now? Who will make the decisions when she can no longer say, 'I'll have to ask my husband.'? The centre point of her day has gone. Equality is too new a state to have removed the fact that, in most marriages, the man comes first, and his likes and dislikes dominate home life from food to fashion. Marriage is very habit-forming, and habits are hard to break.

'Desolation' is a word that is constantly repeated. A lifetime of devotion can have gone into one man: 'How my heart did not stop in 1980, I do not know. Now I live in perpetual purgatory.' This from Mrs Graham Sutherland, widow of the famous painter. 'I still love him, I can't imagine anything that will replace him', the widow of President Sadat wrote. 'If only you knew how hard it has been, how much I have struggled with myself. All through the years, the King always told me everything first. I do so miss that,' Queen Mary told a lady-in-waiting, one year after George V died.

At the opposite end of that empty tunnel, a young mother is now bereft of anyone to share the pleasure and burdens of her growing children. No one but the other parent really cares about the daily happenings of a family world. The single responsibility of parenthood can be awesome. 'I could not be sure I was making the right decision for the children.' Another widow spoke of the 'great weight that had been lifted from my shoulders', when her children reached adulthood.

Regardless of her age, over-reaction of one kind or another seems to be part of the widow's lot. A little tolerance instead of outside pressure and she will eventually revert back to an acceptable normality. That does not necessarily mean she will become the wife/woman others once knew. But relatives who tut their disapproval of her 'drinking', for instance, should try to understand the despair that brought it on. Only if it goes on to become a habit should they become anxious.

Jane Russell admits, in her recent biography, that her state of widowhood caused her to become 'a mad alcoholic – violent and paranoic'. Her rescue came in a return to her religion, and she became a born-again Christian. It could also be that the passing of time – a distancing from the shock – had something to do with it.

Lady Melchett threw herself into work, interests, and parties. 'It may seem strange, surviving by pretending to enjoy life, but you can only be what you are. I hated the idea of being pitied.'

They all find a surfeit of time to be filled in. Yesterday's Sloane Rangers are today's sad widows of Knightsbridge, shopping in Harvey Nichols and Harrods. Some pour their spare love and attention into tiny dogs. However, animals are a tie that not all want in these days of easy travel.

Travel is a time filler as well as an escape. 'Go somewhere', widows are so often told. And yet the tears of a widow who has hardly stopped travelling for twenty years bear out that this is not necessarily the answer. Escape in travel has become a way of life as unsatisfactory as her widowhood. She wants her husband back and cannot reconcile herself to the fact it cannot be.

The need to get on with *something* is strong. There are so many empty days to be filled, because 'It's not their presence you miss but the promise of their return.'

Positive thinking is a great help: 'I made up my mind at the very beginning, I was not going to sit at home and feel sorry for myself.' Very creditable for a widow after forty-three happy years.

Some women embark on a frantic spending spree because of the guilt inherent in having the riches of an insurance policy instead of their husband – or is it that money gained in this way has no value?

'From not ever talking through the past, I now have to think in the past, because he was in the past.' Dates on the calendar are forever marked by past events which will constantly filter into the present. There are days when the staff of the Queen Mother know she will prefer to withdraw from her public round and mark out her appointment-book accordingly.

There are steps along the way, indeed hurdles, which must be taken before the widow can get on with her life and discover: 'Good gracious, I haven't thought of him all morning.'

It is the purpose of this book to explain them.

I

Shock

'People say such stupid things'

'It never crossed my mind we would not die together', Mrs Graham Sutherland commented after death closed fifty-seven happy years of being together. Regardless of whether a marriage is long or short, this is the way most wives see their future.

Even a death that is expected by virtue of a terminal illness is as unexpected as an accident when it actually happens. 'The doctor had said he was a walking time bomb. I just thought the doctor was putting a scare into us', said Hilda. But, sadly, within days she was to write to a friend: 'My poor ole cuddly Maurice died the day before he was to have open heart surgery.'

However much the wife feels she has geared herself for the loss, its impact will not be fully comprehended until it happens. 'I found it a huge struggle to push it back – I can even feel the atmosphere of the hospital room where we all gathered that morning for the surgeon to explain all the dreadful details to us. The same was true of the afternoon as I found myself seeing the face of the head nurse in intensive care – not hearing her voice, but knowing all she had to say' – Hilda.

The widow cannot at first perceive that family and friends are enveloped in the same shock waves. When they stutter stock phrases of comfort to her, they are to some extent consoling themselves. But there are those distanced enough from it to see, for instance, that the widow is: lucky to be free from stress; to have had the good years, the memories; to have shared his success, the children, the house, the career.

Right after it has happened, in those immediate days, a widow cares little about such things. 'In the first few days, all that is really needed is the presence of a comforting voice. I understood when they said, "I don't know what to say", because they did not.'

Women whose husband's work leads him into danger: policemen, servicemen, lifeboat crews and other rescue teams, may have an inner mechanism which shrouds the fear when their man is on duty. However, wives who wave their husbands off to an ordinary day's work rarely do so with any sense of foreboding.

In Susan's case, she had a sense of elation on that particular day. It would be his last day at his workplace, a farewell to his workmates, because he was shortly to be opening his own business.

What every wife fears when her husband is late home from work was a nightmare that came true for Susan – but not immediately. She anticipated he would be late because he had planned to have a few drinks with the lads when they closed shop. Therefore, when midnight came and he was not in, she went to bed.

At 3 a.m. the baby woke her. Even when she realized he was not yet back, she did not panic. She reasoned that he had probably over-celebrated and had had the sense to sleep it off before driving home. When she returned from delivering their older child to school and there was still no sign of him, she decided to phone his place of work. What Susan did not discover until much later was that his friends, in a show of male solidarity, were being evasive in the details they gave her.

Not satisfied, she phoned the police station near the shop. They had nothing to report and suggested she wait until noon before doing anything else. One has to accept that her story of a missing husband was one they were likely to have heard many times before, and one that rarely had an unhappy ending.

Susan herself half-suspected her husband might be in hiding because: 'He was supposed to have a vasectomy that day and might have got cold feet.' After she relinquished that idea, she went to her local police station. There she was to discover that there were no accident details that matched up with him.

As more time went by and she began to worry, she returned. The police told her they did have the body of a man who had been killed on a pedestrian crossing the night before, but he did not match her description. Just in case, though, they first took her home to get a neighbour for company for a visit to the hospital morgue. 'I still thought it was a mistake,' says Susan. A lot of the delay that occurred had been the result of reports that did not tally. But Susan was to discover that the man with no identification – who had been hit by a car – was her husband.

Vicky, a yachtsman's wife, also had an agonizing wait. Her daughter took the first call from the Air Sea Rescue Service, who said: 'We're going to rescue your father.' No one in the family had known he was in trouble. They were expecting him home from a sailing holiday across the Channel. She clung to the telephone seat, trying to convince her daughter and herself he would be all right. 'He was always so careful when sailing.' She would find out later that although he was still attached to the safety clip when he went overboard, he was not clothed warmly enough to resist the icy cold of the rough seas under his oilskins.

The final call came from someone who identified himself as a policeman, but did not pause to find out whether the wife was alone before baldly informing her she was a widow.

From reports of women involved in this book, it is a worrying fact that too often not enough care is taken to cushion the blow. One was simply told: 'Your husband's had a bad turn', and was not even informed which hospital he was in. 'After endless telephone calls I found the hospital and they told me he was dead – could I come later on.' Fortunately, in her case, a colleague at work saw what was happening and took her home. One must remember, even if they scream 'Leave me alone,' they really do need someone to hold them close – to care.

Rose was to have that one advantage – consideration. On Valentine's Day in the 1940s, her life was to change forever. 'He brought me a cup of tea, said, Cheerio, I'll see you later.' 'Later' brought a policeman to her door. 'Your husband's met with an accident.' He helped Rose get a neighbour to watch her children and bring her in-laws to her side. It would be the last kindness she would get from Authority for a long time. At the hospital close to where he worked as a lorry driver: 'They sent me to a desk, a man looked at a paper – no one said how he was.' This was a time when Authority had little compassion; rather it felt it should stay above it. If ever there was a need for another white lie, it would surely have been under these circumstances.

At that time, one did not question Authority, so Rose did as directed and meekly sat on a bench to wait. 'Then two nurses arrived and one said, do you want to see him?' and she knew . . .

Frances Anne, not yet married two years, went to live on a Mediterranean island with her husband, who was teaching there. Ten weeks after their baby was born, the Chief of Police, who had by now become part of their social world, arrived at her door. 'I knew he had something awful to tell me – he was wearing his uniform.' The news was that her husband had been the target of a lone sniper and she was a widow. Even as she was taken to view the body, she could not believe what had happened. 'I convinced myself it was all a plot to confuse the terrorists.' She was sure it was a continuing nightmare that had to end. 'Everything would be all right' – but it wasn't. 'From then on I became paranoid about the baby's safety. I was afraid They would strike again.'

Marie's husband's car crashed within minutes of leaving the house for work. She did not know this until a State Trooper (the equivalent of the British county police) arrived at her door. 'As soon as the State Trooper told me to sit down I knew he was gone. Really, at that time my mind closed a door, and has only opened it a little at a time since. I believe I realized I couldn't stand the shock all at once, so I just carried on.'

Madame El Said had to stifle all her emotions when she was told about her husband's assassination at his father the Prime Minister's side, because her mother-in-law was staying with her. 'In one day, she had lost her husband, her son, country, position and possessions.' When the older woman asked her why she was wearing black, she told her only that the Iraqi Royal family was dead. She kept the Press at bay by saying that she was the maid.

For Jehan Sadat, the horror was instant. She was watching the parade from a balcony when he was assassinated.

No variation of the moment of widowhood is any easier to take. 'When Lyndon died, my immediate response was almost anger. No – not now – later' – Mrs L. B. Johnson, widow of the US President.

Sarah was in hospital for an operation, 'the third of several. This one was successful.' However, bad news was to come. Her son arrived with it, but preferred that the consultant at the hospital be the one to tell his mother.

Joan R., who was living in India at that time, was told that her husband had only six months to live. She decided to keep the news to herself so that their life could go on normally until . . .

Barbara knew, in spite of the warning heart attacks her husband, the playwright Jack Pulman, had suffered, that he was a workaholic and unable to slow down. 'I kept the car at "ready" at all times.' They were preparing to go out to lunch when the final attack came. She managed to get him to the hospital where the doctor had saved him on three previous occasions. This time, he came in tears to tell Barbara he had failed. 'I ended up consoling him instead of the other way round.'

Although her husband had a history of heart trouble, Marina was taken by surprise by the suddenness of his death. 'He had had other operations and come through, and the day before he went into hospital, he sent off a cheque for a holiday for us.' Two days later, Lord Vaizey was dead.

However ill the husband has been, the wife is off guard if she has been told he is getting better. Norma had only recently been telephoned by the hospital and informed he was over the worst of his operation. When she left there a widow, she remembers being furious that everyone other than she and her immediate family were walking around normally.

Joan C. thought her troubles were behind her when her husband recovered from a dangerous illness he had contracted when they were on holiday. Within weeks of being home, he was in hospital in terrible pain – cancer of the liver was diagnosed. She set about investigating clinics where he might be helped. Then a call came for her to hurry to his side. 'It happened so suddenly. The Sister at the hospital gave me a brandy and coffee. While I was having this, I was asked to go down to the office to collect my husband's belongings, as they wanted to go for lunch.'

While one understands that such tragedies cannot be seen by the staff on a personal level, or their jobs would be impossible, there ought to be a better way to deal with widows only minutes away from being wives. The Registrar to whom Joan next went for the Death Certificate was also in such a hurry, he appeared to have lost all sense of feeling. Could he not have seen that the smear of tears identified Joan? Was there a need to ask abruptly, 'Are you the widow?'

Hospitals figure prominently in memories related to husbands' deaths. Yasmine had been to visit her husband and was told he was progressing well. She went off to do some shopping before returning home. There her son was waiting to tell her . . .

Most difficult of all is when it happens at home. Lauren Bacall was not only haunted by the horrors of Humphrey Bogart's last illness, but by the humiliation she felt for him when his body was taken away in a mortician's sack.

Andra's husband was fit enough for his favourite sport of

cricket: 'Passed A.1 by a top heart-specialist – but he died suddenly just after the children left for school one day. I stared down the road and thought, what can I do, who can I send for? I felt really alone.' Would it have helped Andra to call her children back?

Do children soften the blow? Do they make the widow hold on to her control for their sake – should she, or should they, cry together at once? There is always this fear of frightening them. Jane's children came running in from the garden to say they could not stir Daddy, who was 'asleep in the deck chair'. 'I brought them into the house, sat on the couch and cried. Then, I phoned my mother.' It would take her some time to arrive, so Jane phoned a friend who agreed to come over in the interim. She arrived by taxi: 'The driver stayed and made tea. He said he was doing it for my mother. As more and more people began to arrive, he kept on making tea'.

Younger widows may have the comfort of a mother's shoulder to cry on, but this can sometimes be complicated by a mother-in-law who has her own emotions to deal with. A lot of unnecessary stress arises if the two older women fight over who has the right to the most sympathy. In addition, old scores can be settled in the heat of the moment, if the wife has never been the one the mother-in-law would have chosen. 'In the end, it was me being peacemaker', said one young widow.

If the parents are older, there is concern for them if they are in the house at the time of the husband's death. Celia's were visiting her in Florida, neither of them in the best of health. She had to hold herself together for their sake and delayed telling them.

Bette Hill had guests to dinner and half-expected Graham might get home in time for coffee. Then her children ran into the room to tell her there had been an announcement on television that their father's plane had crashed not far away: 'I ran, hell for leather, down the lane towards the road. A police car was on its way up the drive. They knew it was not a good idea for me to go. I struggled with them, but after a wrestling match and banging on the roof of the Panda car they finally got me back to the house.'

'Regret to inform . . .' is a message that goes out in its thousands through every war. 'My reaction was of complete desolation. I felt my life drain away', said a widow of one of the 'First of the Few', Battle of Britain RAF pilots.

'War has wrecked so many homes, I hope it never does that to us,' said Ellen's husband when he was called back into the Reserves for the Korean war. Sadly, that is just what happened. 'Here I was, twenty-four years old, my life seemed shattered.' The very sound of the word 'Korea' still strikes terror when she hears it.

Another Korean casualty was a postman called back in. The telegram with the news of his death arrived at the Sorting Office. 'His workmates could not deliver the bad news, consequently they went to my mother, who contacted my doctor so that he could be present when I read it.'

And wars have a habit of going on and on. 'There was an announcement about the Battle of Goose Green which said casualties were light. People think it's a sprained ankle or something,' says Catherine. She was visiting relatives in Australia to see if it was a country for their future while her husband was in the Falklands. 'Sunday morning, the telephone rang, my aunt answered it and handed the telephone to my uncle. I knew, I thought, that's it. I remember thinking in one breath, why did it have to be Chris, why not someone else? But I couldn't wish what I was suffering on anyone else . . .'

Is the immediate shock of widowhood, with the discovery of a husband's suicide, any easier to take? Instead of someone bringing her the news or being by the bedside watching his life flow away, she is often the first to know. So many men seem to plan their suicides so that their wife will be the one to find them.

Joanna and her husband had begun a normal domestic day. She was pleased that his depressions seemed to be beginning to fade. They breakfasted together, then she went off to a hairdressing appointment. The house seemed strangely quiet on her return. Uneasily, she began to search. The door of the spare bedroom seemed to be jammed. She forced her way in and found him slumped against the door. 'He had used a shotgun'; but she could not take that in right away. 'I thought he was ill.'

On the other hand, Cynthia had watched her husband's depressions get even worse when they returned to the United States. He had lost his job in Europe. Their romance, which had begun like a Doris Day movie, with a blind date in Washington, had been followed by an invitation to join him in Paris. 'It was a magical time.' Back in California, he discovered that at over fifty, getting work was difficult. 'I felt like I was hanging on to a boat in high seas – just didn't know what was going to happen.' She remembers that morning: 'I got up full of energy. Cleaned house, washed my hair, and saw through the window Tom smoking heavily in the garden. "Even the roses haven't come up", he said.' To him, it seemed to link with his failure to get a job.

She tried to reassure him that things would get better when they moved. They had already planned to go to the East coast where prospects were better. When she came out of the dryer, there was no sign of Tom, only a crestfallen dog by his kennel. At first, Cynthia assumed this was because he had been left behind while Tom visited a neighbour. Then, with sudden premonition, she ran into the rose garden: 'He was on the ground, lying on his back, breath coming in gasps. I saw the gun, flew back to the house, hair dangling, curlers half in and half out.' First she telephoned for help, then ran with ice cubes to put round his head. 'I was flying back up and down the steps by the pool shrieking.' When the ambulance arrived, she urged them on: 'Hurry, he's alive, he's fine. Do anything to save him.' Of course, they could not.

However a man has died, it would seem, a meaningless babble of words may be the first barrier to ward off that final blow. Not everyone may know right away. A condolence card which arrived at one woman's house took her by surprise as she read: 'Sympathy for your widowhood'. The Citizens Advice Bureau were presented with what must be one of their most unusual cases when they were asked to find out if this lady's husband had died. She had last seen him storming out of their house after a quarrel. They came back with a report that he had already been cremated. She had to assume that his body had been dealt with by his son from his first marriage.

In my own case, and I shall henceforth be identified by name, I knew nothing of the moment of my first husband's death. The last words I said to him were: 'I'm going to sleep', which had always been my custom when we took a long journey by car, especially at night, which he favoured because there was less traffic on the roads. What stays glued in my mind is us sitting round the kitchen table beforehand, discussing which route to take. As he had been away at sea for some time, he was eager to see his mother before proceeding to our new posting. He did not know that in choosing this detour he was sealing his fate.

A drunken driver of an articulated lorry, taking the wrong side of one of the hairpin bends in the mountains of Tennessee, smashed into us. I was unconscious for several days and do not remember even being told.

2

Grief

'Mike's dead and I'm alive' – defiance or regret?

Many a widow's immediate reaction is to wish the ritual suicide of widows as was once practised in Asia, Africa, America and Australia was still possible. In her precarious state of mind, the lure of the Hindu funeral pyre and what it represents is enticing. Cynthia admits she spent a lot of time in those early days staring at the ocean and contemplating her own suicide.

One widow remembers how she used to wake up screaming, feeling all the strength had been drained from her body: 'My heart was pounding, I was not aware I was dreaming'. She was, in fact, suffering through what she had watched as her husband had died.

Bereft now of the man who meant more to her than anyone else, with whom she had made her own personal history, the widow is stunned. She feels no one has suffered like herself. The word zombie was used by many to describe their state of mind. They automatically carry on with domestic ritual almost as if to convince themselves that what has happened is a bad dream in which they are trapped – it will soon end.

Rose remembers coming back from the hospital and feeling she had to do something: 'So I ironed'. Another woman stumbled upstairs after an associate at work brought her home.

Her husband's pyjamas were still across the bed: 'I folded them up and then didn't know what to do, so I put them under the pillow as usual.'

Andra says: 'For the first week I was numb, nothing seemed to register.' All a widow knows is that she feels life has come to a shattering halt: 'I lurch from day to day. I wake up every morning, still with that feeling of unbelief', wrote one to me. 'It can't be true, yet I know it is true'. Someone else said: 'I am drenched and submerged in the pain of the loss. I cannot bear to visit the grave.'

Marina was 'amazed at the strength of my grief. I've been treated like an adult by people who should have treated me like a child.' Another woman realizes now: 'I didn't know what I was doing. I'd run a bath and it would go cold.' One lady was 'confined to bed for three weeks with temporary paralysis'. Someone else looks back and says: 'We forget that all clichés are rooted in truth. I felt quite literally torn apart. I felt my right side and arm had been ripped away and I used to look down in a kind of wonder and see if they were still there. The pain was so severe and "real" it was "physical".'

The phrase repeated by many whose husbands had been terminally ill is: 'My suffering was for him, that he had been in such tremendous pain and had to die.' And one explained: 'Only a note I received that said "grieving is loving in another key" reached anywhere near my broken heart.'

And yet, in spite of all this extraordinary pain of grief, sadly, mourning is all too often treated by the general public as a weakness, a self-indulgence.

Worse yet is not to recognize that some women are in such a state that there is a reluctance even to pronounce the words: 'My husband is dead.' They feel that if they do not say it, it will not be so. One woman went to the extreme of making her eldest son do all the necessary phone calls to family and friends. Even one who very firmly told herself at once: 'You are a widow' was to find that neither her brain nor her pattern of life could cope with that fact for nearly two years.

There are those who try to remove themselves from everyone. 'I would love to just hide in a corner, do nothing, see no one', wrote Hilda soon after Maurice's death.

Dorothy Lamour did just that: 'I became a recluse. We'd had twenty-five wonderful years. I thought life was over. I just sat around crying.' She was at least helping herself in that respect. Tears provide the best relief. As Katie Boyle said of her early widowhood: 'Every widow must sob completely, uncontrollably. People who have suffocated their feelings and have not been able to cry have invariably cracked up badly later'.

This rejection of the immediacy of the reality has led to the social custom of employing euphemisms. The two most common, 'lost' and 'gone', are almost the worst. One implies carelessness, the other desertion, but are they still preferable to the finality of 'dead'? Some of the other alternatives, such as 'passed away', 'at peace', 'at rest', 'gone to a better life', 'with the Angels', flow easier over the tongue than that one terrible final word.

All too often, those in authority feel it is better to shield the widow and compound the felony by keeping her from seeing the body. However, the wife whose husband walked out of the house safe and well needs not only to know, but to see why he has not returned. 'I put an advertisement in the local paper to find out exactly what had happened – who ran to his aid?' said a woman whose husband had collapsed and died in the street. 'But no one came forward.'

Seeing is believing. It applies at any level of society, which is why, throughout history, there have been ceremonial lying-in-states of heads of government and monarchs. Yet it doesn't always satisfy.

'The undertaker said I could visit. I didn't want to go, and I regret now that I did. I took one look and ran out.' Joan C. found no resemblance to the man she loved. 'I felt I had to escape and do something totally different after that. I went to a local department store and had a facial. I was with strangers there. I didn't have to have any sympathy poured over me.'

Too many feel the need to maintain a stiff upper lip. It is a British disease of inhibition, and a disease of that generation who 'kept things to themselves'. One woman found that not even her mother would let her cry on her shoulder. She had gone through her own widowhood iron-jawed, and expected her daughter to follow suit.

Kathleen Kennedy suffered in a similar way for different reasons. She was visiting her family in New York when the news came that the Englishman she had married had been killed in the fighting in Europe in the Second World War. A friend who broke through the barrier of relatives asked if she had been given a sleeping pill. 'No,' Kathleen confessed. 'My mother just keeps taking me to Mass and saying that God sends us no cross heavier than we can bear.' Her wedding had caused great disapproval because the Marquis of Hartington was a Protestant. Now her mother tried to convince her that she had committed a sin in this marriage, so that, in addition to losing a husband, she was worried about losing her soul. The family motto was: 'Kennedys don't cry.' Therefore, while her sisters and brothers comforted Kathleen, at no time was she given the opportunity to shed tears.

It is a pity that this perfectly natural feeling cannot be more generally recognized as a part of mourning which should not be repressed. There is a lot to commend the Irish Wake, the Jewish Shiva or the Shi-ite Muslim mourning party. They all encourage the widow to 'let go'. A great deal of criticism was levelled at Jehan Sadat and she was seen to be 'westernized' because she followed her husband's cortège calm and controlled. It can be detrimental to expect a grieving person to follow a particular behaviour pattern, nor does it follow that she does not shed tears in private. Regardless of how much weeping and wailing is done at the beginning, it also does not mean that the widow will never cry again. It can be years before that 'time, place or song' ceases to cloud the eyes with memories.

Generally, it is better to do it early on. Much better to be able to admit with retrospective satisfaction: 'I was banging my head against the wall and wailing'; 'My in-laws walked in at the door and we all howled'; 'My training as a Bereavement Counsellor meant at least that I understood what was happening to me and how important it was for us (her daughters and his parents) to grieve together'. No woman should convince herself that she should stay in control for the children's sake. The reasons offered are barriers which they do not want removed.

At first, Bette Hill bottled up her emotions and made herself physically ill. Then she took to the road: 'I remember driving along screaming out of the window, "I don't believe this is happening to me". It was a therapeutic outburst which made me feel light again.'

A friend recounts how Susan Hayward, the Forties' film star, locked herself in the bathroom and yelled her lungs out for ten minutes. When she emerged, she was composed enough to carry on calmly through the rest of the formalities.

Marie says: 'A friend told me to put on one of Robert's sweaters and go outside and scream myself silly. This helped a lot.' Not everyone has the advantage of such a large acreage as hers where no one will hear them. It is the fear of bringing the neighbours running that will stop many a woman from 'letting go'.

Lauren Bacall related in her book *By Myself*: 'I wish I could have stood in the middle of the room and just screamed – screamed until there was no scream left.'

Certain circumstances can, however, prevent a woman from allowing herself the luxury of falling apart. In the Second World War, in order to prevent possible panic at the loss of the longest serving President in US history, his widow Eleanor Roosevelt was required to make an immediate calm statement to the public: 'I am more sorry for the people of this country and the world than I am for ourselves.' Only then, with her duty done, could she retire to mourn with her family.

Jackie Kennedy was determined to stay in control of the

funeral arrangements after her husband was assassinated. Having looked back through the documents in the White House, she was not about to be pushed aside like one of her predecessors, Mary Lincoln. However, the sight of his possessions, such as his rocking-chair, being summarily dispatched from the White House must have been difficult to endure.

Catherine had no time to think, as she was hurried back to England from Australia under the protective shield of Service friends. The Australian army had swung into action and made sure that she had someone known to her at every stop on the route back. The fact that she was nursing her baby gave her something important on which to concentrate. 'It was the only thing that kept me going.' When she arrived at her home in Farnborough: 'The majority of those women who rallied round still had husbands in danger.' How could she let them down or frighten them with her own emotions?

The need to care for her baby was what kept Frances Anne together during her husband's funeral. The final straw had snapped when she had had to take a clean shirt and trousers to the funeral parlour because the ones he had been wearing when he was shot were bloodstained. She had the support of a Serving Sister she had met in the hospital where she had had her baby until her mother arrived to take her back to England.

Like many another woman, Celia was faced with planning her husband's funeral when she had never even attended one before. The process of burial in the United States tends to be cold and businesslike. The widow is faced with a dazzling array of coffins from which to choose. Because of her husband's love of sailing, she went for something simple in wood – 'like a boat'. She then had to decide whether the coffin would remain closed or be opened during the time the mourners visited. In America, the family receive by the coffin in the undertaking establishment, which can have a variety of beautifying names all of which remove it from the taint of 'Death'.

She concentrated on a simple obituary for the local paper.

When it was published, she was horrified to discover that someone had contacted the paper to change the wording to include the claim he was the deceased's best friend. 'I don't understand how people can do such things'. This thoughtless tampering with a widow's tender emotions is all too prevalent.

The funeral proved too much. After the service she went straight to her car. 'I could not shake hands with everyone and thank them for coming'. Nor did she remember much of the rest of that day. 'I felt like somebody else was doing everything'. She is left with regrets of her rushed decision on the burial arrangements. 'Victor was a water person and here we are in the middle of Florida with no water around. They didn't fully inform me of all the facilities of that cemetery. I found out later there was a mausoleum. That would have been better'.

Colonial India had the same dangers from gossip as a small village, so that Joan R.'s husband discovered the truth of his terminal illness. This gave him a few extra months' lease of life. He was determined to get his financial affairs in order. He died just before the partitioning of India. She was advised to leave as quickly as possible because he had been involved in Intelligence work and there was a danger of retribution on his family. Along with other frantic expatriates waiting to get out, she was crowded into a transit camp to await a boat. It was the survival of her three small children that was uppermost in her mind.

Pamela was so badly injured in the car crash that killed her husband that her son could only identify her by a bracelet. 'I was taken to hospital by ambulance. One of the drivers of the cars that stopped had brought in my son. He was not badly injured. I learned later that since, at that moment, no one knew if I would live, he gave him $5 (much more then than it is today) in case he needed some immediate cash. When they had pieced me together, my scalp stitched, jaw wired up, a cast from armpits to thighs, there was some doubt if I would ever walk again. I was too drugged to be aware of much at all, but I do remember my constant confusion: was it my husband or my son who was dead?'

If a husband's death is related to some newsworthy event, or he or his widow are well-known personalities, for them the privacy of tears is at a premium. For instance, upon her husband's assassination, Mrs Cory Aquino immediately became the symbol of the rallying forces of the opposition to Marcos. She had to show a stalwart face to her public and, like many in a similar position, could not even visit the grave in private. Photographers were always there.

Elizabeth Taylor, probably the most beautiful and well-known widow of 1958, was offered little understanding of the fact that she was a young woman of twenty-six who had lost the man she adored. 'I thought I'd never love again'. His funeral was turned into a spectacle of gawping fans with no respect for her grief. They crushed against the windows of the car, almost overturning it as they begged: 'Smile, Liz,' as if this was just one more performance.

Did she remember that stress in later years? It would appear so, but much as she tried not to overshadow Richard Burton's widow Sally at his memorial service in London, the Press would not let her. Sally Burton's problem was one which other widows of previously married men suffer. A squabble can break out among ex-wives as to who has the greatest claim on grief.

Cynthia went through a lot of problems caused by her husband's first wife. This made the funeral arrangements difficult. 'Because Tom had been a war hero, it was proposed that he have a military funeral.' This meant all the trappings of a riderless horse, caisson (gun carriage) and Marine escort. She was lucky that the hostility towards her did not extend to his son, who agreed to be her escort. 'I remember it through the haze of the car. It wiped me out.'

Unknown women can become spotlighted widows: 'Six months of almost non-stop publicity was hard to bear', said the widow of a policeman killed in the spectacular line of duty. This kind of woman has nowhere she can retreat to and pretend, at least for a while, that it never happened. There is no equivalent to a new High Street, where she can shop free from questions. Her picture is plastered over every paper, so that more than just neighbours know her story. She has to face up to it at once. This can never be her personal tragedy; public demands come first.

There is, however, one bonus: they have an opportunity they would never normally enjoy of making their feelings known. A working coal-miner's widow could scream her blame on the strike for his suicide and see it carried across several headlines.

While there is no one rule for easing the pain, being able to talk is of prime importance. 'It helps to talk about him. To have to stop would eliminate an important part of my life.' Sadly, not enough people want to listen. It becomes an embarrassment to those who call: 'I wanted to talk about my husband, but everyone avoided the subject'. 'Well-wishing friends and relatives shunned the subject with as much energy as if my innocent husband had committed some unspeakable crime.'

Two women were able to solve this problem because they originally met at their respective husbands' bedsides in the hospital. 'We would have never met but for this, but it has proved the basis of our friendship. We can talk to each other about them.'

However, if she talks to a close male friend of the family who shares the loss, this can be quickly expanded into a romance. This is tragic, because the widow has a genuine need to be with people who appreciated her man; who knew him well enough to reminisce – smile, yes, smile at past events; be ready with that extra little supportive phrase that can mean so much. One woman had this comfort snatched away from her in an ugly scene in which she was accused of encroaching on a female friend's 'territory'.

Cynthia took her husband's best friend to visit him at the cemetery. 'We got wine and sandwiches to have a Wake for Tom. Someone passing reported us to the Authorities, complaining "People are carrying on at the grave."' While passers-by may have felt the dignity of Arlington Cemetery was being disturbed, one must accept that the bereaved have a right to do as they please, within reason. She felt that 'Tom would have enjoyed us being there'. Even more important was the end result. This friend told Cynthia that the happiness and understanding she had given Tom had added ten years to his life.

The right words are so very important. Although Andra had an unknown vicar at her husband's funeral service, 'He had done his homework and the address really helped me. I walked out of the church less stressful.' This is in contrast to the experiences of many widows who have had to suffer a non-interested minister droning through stock phrases.

What widows are most unprepared for is the fact that sympathetic ears close with an almost audible snap. The widow goes from: 'Within six hours the house was full of people and it stayed that way for two months' to – Silence. Too many assume, after the polite condolence call has been made, that the widow will now get on with her life. They rarely check back to find out if she has. In any case, should she continue to lean in their direction, too many have been slapped back smartly. It is as well not to take 'Let me know if you want anything' too seriously. As one said: 'I soon learned the truth of that old adage – "A friend in need is a pain in the arse."'

It was summed up by another woman: 'Friends could easily be divided into the few who stayed supportive and the many who offered one dutiful invitation to dinner, one dutiful invitation to the theatre, and that was that.'

However, there are plenty of women who would say that these several crumbs from the table were to be envied. They were not even offered a bare board.

One of the most hurtful things the majority of widows suffer is the sight of people so obviously crossing the road to avoid them. This can only be assumed to be a selfish fear on their part of having to deal with the possible distress a kind word will bring. Thus in the desperate early days she finds that not only is her prop in life removed, but her surrounding supports go as well, and it hurts.

Marina has realized: 'If I draw on my resentment, that way lies madness. I know I'm ultra-sensitive. People have genuine feelings about widows. They come to the surface and you must tell yourself, it's not me, it's my status as a widow.'

And so the majority find it works better to keep their grief to themselves. 'I went back to work,' Andra says, 'which was very hard, as people trying to be kind end up avoiding you. Luckily, I was in a job where I could have a little weep and no one would notice.'

The last word on those tears comes from Barbara Cartland. 'When you cry, you are crying for yourself, not for them.' Like one third of the world, she follows the philosophy of Buddha. 'I don't believe in death. They are there with you always.'

The majority of widows have a Circle of Grief which they have to complete before they can come to terms in any way with their situation. Only they know its true circumference. It involves those she feels must be told. This does not always include those who first come forward, which is why it can take a while for her to get round to all of them – telling them herself – grieving with them. It has driven women across oceans, even half-way round the world and closer to home, through every page in every address book she ever owned. Once she has done this, there will be a subtle change in her outlook.

3

The first year – 'is hell'

It is generally agreed that the first year is the worst. It is a year in which searing pain, utter desolation and despair become familiar companions. Looking back at the previous year, the widow is bound to remember all the little things she and her husband did together. Every action gains a sense of poignancy: 'I was very emotional and completely shattered during the first year, in spite of knowing for some time that Paul was going to die soon. I think pre-death strain took its toll after. The wound is now healed but the scar will stay forever.'

The small, everyday reminders of a widow's loss are perhaps the most difficult. The garden her husband tended that blooms on without him. Her neighbour's husband's washing on the line. The car waiting in the garage. The pipe rack. The drawers full of his clothes. Letters that continue to arrive addressed to him. And the nightly reminder of that extra pillow on the bed.

The wealth of advice a widow is given at this time can be more of a problem than a help. First and foremost, the timing is all too often wrong – she is in no condition to absorb it, let alone judge what applies best to her. In the first days and weeks, all that is needed is a comforting voice and presence. So often, what a widow gets are such statements as: 'Of course, you don't need such a large house any more.' This is a debate to be reserved for a later date and not to be taken seriously, unless she discovers her finances have fallen apart. Such advice often precipitates a move before she has recovered sufficiently to know what she really wants, and leads to a lot of unnecessary regrets later on.

During those months which make up that first year, often in the initial most shattering weeks, a widow, at her most vulnerable, is called upon to make decisions about her home and children's future which require thought and deliberation. This she is incapable of doing, right then.

Income Tax forms descend ruthlessly before she is able even to think logically. Widows are often also required to settle or approve business affairs when they do not, at this time, really wish to be reminded that life must go on.

However inhumane these actions from authorities may seem, they do produce advantages. The widow is forced to divert her thoughts and energy elsewhere. Anger raised by such seeming callousness can usefully blunt the sharpest edge of her grief. So can the anger directed against 'Them' – the doctors who should have known, warned, advised earlier; the person who caused the accident; the 'why me?' of the victim left behind.

Soon after Catherine returned to England, she went to her family in the north for a memorial service for her husband, but she then chose to continue to live in the south. 'You'll always visit your family, but if you live too far away from friends, it is easy to lose touch.' She was, of course, still intent on clinging to the edges of the life she had led with Chris.

She then had the opportunity to visit the Falklands. Chris's father and her mother went with her. 'It was important to see where he had died.' Several of the Paras stationed there were old friends. Service people, being family unto themselves, can stretch rules. One of them, a helicopter pilot, flew Catherine over the battleground. 'It is marked with cairns where the men had fallen.' Later she went with the families to the actual area and for a while was separated from the others. 'I walked over the ground alone and it was very special.'

Pamela was also under the protection of the services, in her case the US Navy, who took over all the formalities connected with her husband's death and the funeral. 'Friends who were travelling in that area at the time heard about the accident on the radio and came to the hospital to see what they could do to help. By then my son was able to travel, so they took him back to his grandparents in Illinois. I was still in a very poor condition, my mouth was wired together, eating was impossible except from the tip of a spoon, there were constant sessions with the physiotherapist and decisions had to be made about where the treatment would continue when I finally left hospital – where would I live? We had been on a transfer and by now all our furniture had arrived in Norfolk, Virginia. That first year passed in a blur.'

Frances Anne was also having problems of adjustment. Her mother opened a boarding house on the coast and she offered to help run it, then: 'I was riding on a bus in Manchester when I read in the paper that the terrorist who had killed my husband had been acquitted.' She became fearful, somehow, that 'they' would strike back at her.

Cynthia retired in total misery to her mother's home. The family rallied round. 'My sister painted his portrait.' She would walk the beaches nearby, thinking thoughts of her own suicide.

Some were forced, like Yasmine and Bette Hill, into having to adjust down their living standards quicker than they would have wanted. They represent many who discovered their financial pot was not as full as they expected.

Unhappily, when a widow is ready to re-enter the ordinary world, she has often come to the end of her state as a 'nine-day wonder', and finds to her astonishment that she is faced with a complete change of attitude. Plain advice is now hard to come by, and there is a dramatic change in her social position. One woman has been more fortunate because of the status of certain close friends: 'The people who have been extremely solicitous have been three gay couples. If any widow knows a stable gay couple, they are lucky. One isn't a threat to them and they are not to you – so it works.'

Some newly-raw widows have been kind enough to share their feelings about this earliest part of their widowhood. So much happens that makes a widow wonder if she has lost her mind as well as her husband. To know that she is not unique in that feeling may help.

A lot of the quotations that follow may seem disjointed and unrelated. They exemplify the way a widow feels during those first weeks or months of shock.

When her husband died, Joan C. was completely on her own, with neither children nor parents. There was not even a job to lose herself in, since her husband had recently persuaded her to give it up and begin again as a freelance. Joan is a photographer. Business had yet to come in in any quantity, so she sat at home, very much alone. 'I was convinced I would feel better after the funeral, but it was not so, I ached even more.'

Work began to come in slowly. The work was mostly with strangers, and it brought the compensation of being removed from answering questions or needing to admit to the widowhood she was still unready to accept. Joan fights against tears in public. She used to dodge neighbours rather than embarrass them with her grief. She shopped away from familiar streets, finding it distressing every time she bought 'for one'. The most soothing thing in her life at that time was to play over and over the tape of her husband's cremation service, at which an old friend had given a wonderful address.

A temporary rescue came with an invitation to spend Christmas in America. She determined to clear away her husband's clothes before she left: 'I couldn't come home to them.' The visit did not assuage her grief. Joan returned still feeling absolutely lost. 'I asked myself if I was on the edge of a nervous breakdown. It was horrible, frightening, there was nobody depending on me now.'

As she lived through the early, difficult weeks, Joan sought the help of CRUSE, a counselling group for widows about which further- information will be found in a later chapter. She preferred the counsellor to come to her home. 'At first, I just sat and cried.' But now Joan is slowly beginning to look forward again. She has begun to try to do something positive for herself and make new friends. She is trying to sort out some of her husband's manuscripts. He was the author, Denis Cleary. There is an unfinished book and a play that needs some revision.

Unfortunately other people, a neighbour and a business associate close by, have also lost partners, and because they feel she is ahead of them in the pattern of grief she is expected to be the one to offer consolation. 'But it is hard, and sets me back again.'

Marina and her husband had never sat down and had a serious 'if' conversation. 'I tried to, but all I got was, "You'll be all right." He had left a file of instructions. I both did and didn't know it was there.' This, of course, is all part of the wife's pattern of preferring not to think in that direction. She says: 'The alteration in my status has yet to sink in. I'm no longer part of John's world. His political life is gone. I used to go to the House of Lords to watch him speak'. John was Lord Vaizey.

She feels she owes her career to him. She has a weekly column in a Sunday newspaper. 'Most career women who are married have their husband's support, both mental and financial. Now it has been snatched away. I expected to be able to carry on normally, and I haven't at all.' Marina has found: 'My career is on hold. Even my emotions are in suspense.'

Dealing with a lack of perception comes hard to widows, even though the understanding may be there. 'When something devastating has happened to you, you cannot expect other people to act out of character.'

It would be as well for the outsider to realize that shock not only turns a woman temporarily into another person, but that she will never be exactly the same again.

Marina is resentful of those who have not been in touch with her, the ones she now clearly sees were only part of her husband's life. Added to the emotional stress have come problems with her Georgian house: dry rot, damp and woodworm. 'The house is chaotic – behaving the way I feel. If life is swings and roundabouts, this is a rollercoaster.'

Marie looks back on her first year with great clarity.

'I still find it very difficult. At first I prayed that it wasn't true, even believed that that was possible. His last words to me were, "kiss me goodbye".' What made it even weirder for Marie was that during the afternoon before he died, Robert had said, almost prophetically: "No matter what happens, I'll always be with you."

'I'd dream he was in the house, hear him call me and talk to me. Having to telephone everyone did help. I had to repeat the story so many times and was so horrified at the shock I must be causing, things got turned around. I became the comforter – it was strange.

'It has never really come into my mind: "I'm a widow." Most peculiar, I feel alone, lonely, many times unloved, sometimes even deserted. The first night I didn't sleep, the second day and night I drank a lot and looked at many photograph albums of Robert and me. After that, I took each day as it came. My doctor was a lifesaver – he saw me once a month, just for moral support. I could cry, laugh, talk or do nothing – he was better than any shrink.'

Marie found comfort in visiting the cemetery often – sometimes even at night when she couldn't sleep. 'I talked to Robert and felt that he was helping me – I couldn't believe he was dead. I believe he is always with me and always will be, which makes it difficult to believe that I'm a widow.

'On my first wedding anniversary, after he died, which would have been our 25th, I bought a ticket (I was going to say tickets) to *Evita*, booked a hotel room, saw the show, had a lovely dinner with all the trimmings, then ordered breakfast in bed for next morning as we always had. I enjoyed it even though I was lonely – I felt as if I was going ahead with my life. When people asked me what I was going to do, since I have no children, I told them I was going to be Auntie Mame and put all my dressy clothes in a trunk and travel round visiting all my nieces and nephews.'

Marie's widowed sister, who came over to help her through the first weeks, had dealt with her own situation differently. She told Marie to get rid of all her fancy dresses and feather boas because there would be no need to wear them any more.

'My answer was, "Well, dammit, if I can't wear them anywhere else, I'll wear them at home." Which I have done, many times. Whenever I have a party, all the finery comes out – I don't care if everyone else comes in jeans. I've always liked to dress up, and Robert encouraged me.'

Robert had been a musician playing in the piano bar of an elegant restaurant. Facing squarely one of the most difficult of ordeals, Marie went there alone and made herself go through all the things they had done together. She even sat on one of the stools around the edge of the grand piano in just the same way – and survived the test.

On the day her husband had died, the bank had sent a guard round to Celia's home. One can understand their concern; Celia was now alone in a mansion in Palm Beach which was known to be filled with exquisite antiques. Also, she was in line to inherit approximately 200 million dollars. And, shortly after her husband's death, she had to deal with the tactless stupidity of a so-called friend whispering, 'Spend it,' as a form of condolence.

She had no chance to retreat into solitude. The day after the funeral she had to go to the bank. 'They wanted to know if I had the key to the vault.' Celia's husband has told her little about his business affairs. 'I always told him, don't leave me without a bottle of milk, leave me a note somewhere, but he didn't.' She was not even aware who had the legal ownership of the cars. Right away, an immediate search had to be made through files and papers. 'Going into his office was strange. There on the board were still his new ideas for inventions. I sat in his chair, something I'd never done before. It was ripped and patched. He'd covered it with an old towel. I had bought him a new chair some time earlier, but he had sent it back.'

Besides being a successful inventor, Victor Farris had also been a businessman. 'He had seventeen corporations'. He had been about to close a large real estate deal just before his death. The other participants were now worried it would fall through. 'They asked me if I was part of the corporation. The man asking the questions was trying to be sweet, not frantic.' A search revealed she was listed as secretary of the corporation and therefore in a legal position to sign cheques. 'They all heaved a sigh of relief. After that I was signing things till I was cross-eyed.'

This was not to be the end of her immediate involvement in his business affairs. Another deal had gone through which now had a tax bill due. 'I wrote a cheque for two million dollars – I wanted to know exactly where I stood.' One important piece of advice her husband had always impressed on Celia was not to trust anyone. Widowed friends who came to visit reiterated that advice. It all helped when she was deluged with phone calls about the business, the sale of the boat, the cars. At that time, she could not even bring herself to get into his Rolls Royce or board the yacht. 'I put a captain in charge to keep it in trim.'

All she managed to do at the beginning was to enter his bedroom to collect some treasures to put in hers. 'The money clip I gave him when we were first married. A belated Valentine card I sent him which he still had on the shelf, a painting I'd done of him when we were first married.' Everything else could wait.

Hilda could not understand why she, the dependable, reliable mother, was not acting that way any more. She had yet to realize that without her Maurice, she was not the same person. Her children, swept up in their own grief at the loss of their father, were unable to give her the help she needed. No one in the family seemed to be able to look at problems impartially. One has to accept that at times like this no one is acting rationally. Unkind things are said and regretted. Decisions are made that are totally wrong. There is no practice for a situation like this to make it perfect.

All the following quotations come from a series of Hilda's letters which began when Maurice died.

At first, she was attempting to push back reality. By keeping her grief immediate, she felt closer to her husband. When a daughter tried to make her realize the passage of time, Hilda just put her hands over her ears and refused to listen. Another temporary solution was to recreate situations they had shared.

'I drove his blue truck today and felt very close to him – nobody knows that I took it out, or that I drove along Broadway just as we had done so many times together. It all seems so dumb as we both just went together. It was always Maurice and Hilda and it still should be the same and to me it is, but letters bring only my name now and it seems so odd. He will always be with me, even though I feel apart, on my own, yet I play the game (I suppose I do) that he is still with me. Maybe it helps me to play this game. I don't know. I guess it will suffice until inside myself I feel ready to accept what I am supposed to accept. Maybe I don't ever have to accept it as long as I carry on in a reasonable manner and don't start talking to him when he is not here, so that people feel that I have gone nutty. I am very sane, that's for sure.'

Time passed, but Hilda's anguish continued and was exacerbated as the year was about to change. 'I am not happy about him being left in 1984. One of the yells that the cheerleaders chant in a football game, especially if the opposing team is near the scoring line, is – "Push'em back". That's the way I feel about the New Year.'

Even someone else's handwriting in the order book in the business that was Hilda's livelihood caused unreasoning resentment. It was an intrusion into her efforts to escape reality. 'I want it still to be yesterday. If the pain was less with time, maybe I could feel differently about it. I would love to say, "Hooray, I feel no pain." Do I subconsciously feel that he is with me all the time or is it that I just want him to be and make it that way?'

Hilda is an Englishwoman, a long time resident in Texas, and when crisis struck it was to her English family that she instinctively turned. They were an important part of her marriage. They had been with her when she first met Maurice. It was only through one brother's intervention that she ever received her father's permission to marry. But now they were far away. The need to grieve with them was impossible to satisfy. She had to stay close to home, keeping the business going.

As she was to discover, nothing she could do would hold back time. The date of the anniversary of her husband's death came and she recorded her feelings: 'All of us went to the cemetery that night. We took beautiful roses, but I had asked that we only stay long enough to arrange them. Had I been free all day to go out, it would have been a much different evening.' Hilda, still acting as good old Mum, even if she did not recognize it, had agreed to wait for the family until they came in from work. 'I myself wanted to keep going to the cemetery, and I am sure that I would have done that, not once during the day, but many times – and even, I feel, to his hospital room. I feel that I may have torn out to the hospital, as I get that urge on and off – I see him there, smiling and laughing, and I suppose that is how I want him to be. His clothes are still hanging – I had thought that I might put them in storage boxes, but I can't.

'Come to think of it, I am just the same way at the cemetery. I look at his marker, but I won't or don't really see his name. I have come to the conclusion that while everything of Maurice's is still here, I feel he is here, because I want him to be – it has been a year, but it is like today to me. He is at the hospital, but I really don't want him to appear in my mind as being there. I am glad he is out of pain now, and maybe I am being selfish to want him back. No, I only want him back if he can be well.

'I will look forward now, I must and I will be a new me in time. I have said this to myself so many times and really meant it at that time, but I realize that it just cannot be an overnight thing. Someday I will wake to the fact that it is easier. I think it will be easier before I realize that it has been easier. Does that make sense? I say this because I have started laughing again at things and didn't realize that I had done so until maybe even a few days later, when it dawned on me that I was not quite the zombie on that certain day – it must creep in, at a slow pace, as some power knows that it is best for one this way. The always feeling in limbo is for a reason, as your mind stays dull and does not let you think – that is good, as your inside really is healing without you knowing, until the time comes that you can safely face what has happened without going crackers.'

This period of time is summed up by someone else: 'The first anniversary of that dreadful day of death, and you live again for the umpteenth time the shock and the horror and the immediacy of the loss. Though it is, can it be worse than any other day now?'

4

Emptiness – helplessness

'There was nothing to do – nothing, I used to lie in bed and cry.'

How long does it take to get used to the silence of a telephone when a husband used to call several times in his working day? If you have lived by the motto: 'Cuddles are important', what does one do? It is all very well for the outsider to say, 'Pull yourself together': this takes time.

The widow is abruptly cut off from a sharing relationship. The truth is trying to force its way through and is meeting a wall of rejection. 'They didn't understand the way I was feeling and thought I was only being awkward (which I was)', said one woman of her family. They cannot possibly be as acutely aware as she of how poignant is everything she does: once they did this together. 'There are days when the pain sweeps in and it seems no better. Something I see on TV, a country scene, green fields and trees which we loved to go to together.'

Marie says: 'There will never again be for me that wonderful warmth and security that comes from being truly loved by an unselfish human being. I miss his touch, the warmth of his smile, the laughter in his eyes – the joy of knowing him. I miss feeling special – feeling beautiful and desired. Without him, I feel incomplete and somehow feel that my personality has suffered. He wasn't perfect, but he was perfect for me.'

Cynthia had retreated to her mother's home. 'All I did was

lie there and tremble. I didn't sleep at night.' A widow has no one to turn to. 'There is no one to discuss things with. No one to tell, you don't feel so hot today': a luxury reserved for a wife, not a widow. 'Things were blurry for a year or more after Richard died' – June Allyson.

Mary was awarded an OBE for her work in Social Services. She had done pioneer work in getting early immigrants accustomed to their new life and later worked among students during the riotous days of the 1960s. By the time she went to the Palace to collect that OBE, she was a widow of a month. 'His name was down as my guest. It all passed in a blur.'

As Joan C.'s husband had worked from home, she now faced coming in to an empty house. 'Life has no direction for me any more. I really do not care. It seems ridiculous, I was so busy and independent and a tower of strength, now I'm so helpless. I didn't realize I needed him so much. There is no one to come home to. I feel I was suddenly forced into this situation without any preparation or warning. You think it will never happen to you but it does. I asked myself if I was on the edge of a nervous breakdown. It was horrible, frightening, there was nobody depending on me now.' She also spent a lot of time worrying: 'Shall I forget him and all the things we shared?'

Mary Hemingway recounted in her book how: 'Going to bed was the toughest part for me. Not so much for the cuddling but the bedtime talk, the comfort. I starved for the smell of Ernest's chest where my nose always muzzled. I ached to touch his skin which was smoother than any other; having no creature to absorb and appreciate pats, hugs, kisses, I floundered in a void of unexpressed affections and I missed my husband daily.'

If the couple have worked together, it can be even worse. Diana Raymond and her husband were both writers and had worked in the same office. She had turned to him for editing and advice. Now, she found herself constantly asking: 'What am I doing in here by myself?'

Well-meaning employers of couples who have shared a

position often insist the widow come back. This is not likely to be successful. It was one thing to work with her husband as steward and stewardess at the British Legion, but the widow of one of the men lost in the Mumbles lifeboat disaster found the responsibility more than she could manage alone.

Yoko Ono, who had resented losing her own identity when John Lennon was alive, is now quite happy to be known as Mrs Lennon. It is also interesting to note that, in widowhood, she has gained a lot of respect from the fans who originally blamed her for the break-up of the Beatles. 'Suddenly, I'm loved; I'd rather have John back and be hated again.'

For the wife who has happily spent most of her days in the home, it is no longer her haven. 'I found I wanted to be out of it. For six months I ran, my feet hardly touched the ground.' The need to get out of the house is commonplace. One lady who prided on her homemaking as a wife, deserted her house to dirt as a widow. She chose instead to cook, clean, wash and sew in her brothers' homes. 'I ran from one to the other.' Fortunately, they had wives who were willing to humour her.

Weekends make their isolation even more acute. Outside, couples are pottering around doing all the things she can no longer share. Everyone is too busy to give her any of their time. Joan C. solved this by grabbing any weekend photographic assignments on offer: 'My married colleagues were never interested in them.' Another woman overcame those dreaded hours when she would have been preparing dinner for her husband, by taking a part-time job in a nearby Technical College. 'That was when they needed someone to help in their bookshop – it suited me perfectly.'

During this very tender time, the widow can be faced with the harshness of authority. Rose needed some immediate assistance and was sent to the Pensions Office. 'I explained I had no income and two small children, rent etc.' They sent her to what was then called the Public Assistance Office. 'A man there said they could only give me a card for groceries. No other immediate help. I couldn't believe this was happening.'

Rose had bitter memories of her own mother's struggle after the First World War left her a widow.

As if that was not enough, she had to attend the inquest into her husband's accidental death (he had run into the path of a lorry). She remembers: 'The driver was there. I felt sorry for him, he was in such a state. I wanted to go up to talk to him, but the solicitor said "no"'. So do cold legal minds prevent the few words which could make so much difference. Could that solicitor not have recognized that Rose wanted to offer comfort, not to apportion blame? It was a contact from which both would have benefited.

Pamela, now freed from the cast and allowed out of hospital in a brace of similar proportions, had no home to which she could return. 'As a Naval family, we had always lived in quarters or rented a house off Base. As we were between assignments when this accident happened I had nowhere to go which I could claim as my own. In any case I was in no fit state to set up a home of my own yet.' While staying with friends, she insisted on attending the Court when the man who caused the accident was to appear. 'I wanted to see him, but I wasn't sure what I would do when I did.' As it happened, the lawyer pleaded illness on his behalf so he did not attend. Sadly, what did happen was that one of the witnesses present told her what everyone else had been at pains to hide; the extent of her husband's injuries. 'What concerned me most was whether my son had seen him. I was most relieved to discover someone had kept him back from the wrecked car.'

Joanna was required to attend an inquest in connection with her husband's suicide. 'The policeman who had first come to the house was there. I said "Good morning" to him, quite politely, and he looked away and I was hurt.' While one can understand that officialdom must take a detached stance, even a short smile of acknowledgement would go a long way with a woman at such a difficult time.

In too many cases, the widow seems to be a nuisance and is treated accordingly, perhaps none more badly than President

Lincoln's widow, Mary, who was not only excluded from the plans for his funeral, but cut off from funds. This left her badly in debt. She had not only to make her own way but to pay for the extensive wardrobe she had bought in anticipation of the continuation of her life at the White House.

Authority on both sides of the Atlantic seems short on compassion. A widow who had been living in America before her husband died had yet to collect her immigration card. 'As I told the official what had happened, he snatched back the card and told me, "As a widow, you don't get it."'

Just when the widow thinks she might be beginning to have got herself together, she can be caught unawares by the simplest things. Music they shared presents difficulties. Few can manage actually to play favourite records for a long time. There have been reports of quite a number of them smashed in utter frustration. One who did manage to start playing what they had both enjoyed, heard only a few bars before the music was drowned in her sobs. It can spill out of the radio before they can stop it. 'When I hear "Because I love you", I have a little weep,' says Sarah of the song that became 'theirs' from courting days onward.

Those who are blessed with perceptive, caring children at this time have a great advantage. Hilda's daughters continue to scheme how to get her to eat. Either they bring her various dishes 'to try' or find a pretext to share a meal with her or she is taken out – after an argument. 'They try and make me feel ashamed by saying, "Mother, let's stop playing these silly games at not eating."'

A concerned call from her daughter pushed Marjory into confessing she did not think she could continue to live alone. She was finally convinced she was staying too isolated in her misery, but: 'I began crying all the time. I once had to run home from Sainsbury's.' Nevertheless, she made a New Year's Resolution to start to do things. But this was not to last long: she suffered a heart attack and was told to take life quietly for three months. 'Not advice I welcomed', she said wryly. No sooner was she recovered than she fell downstairs and was on crutches for weeks, then went on to contract an infection of the muscles. Quite understandably, Marjory rates that 'a rotten year.'

Ill-health seems to stalk the widow. It could be psychosomatic, or it could be that all her defences are down. All the aches and pains she may have disregarded as a wife can now be given free rein because there is no other purpose to her life. There are numerous accounts of accidents, operations and other calamities. Yasmine fell down a flight of stairs rushing to keep the job she now desperately needed to survive. A long stay in hospital finished her chances there. One said: 'I had an operation and a heart attack and realized how much I was on my own. When you are ill, it is your partner who gives you that extra touch of sympathy.'

The change in her social position is equally hard to accept. Once neighbours have fulfilled their condolence calls the widow is taken aback to find an invisible but definite 'keep off' sign on their fences. She will be surprised to discover how often she is seen as a predator. 'What I needed was the stimulus of male conversation, no more, no less, but it was never construed that way.' 'My friend used to phone when her husband was away on business and say, "Come round". Finally I refused and told her she should invite me when he was home as she had done when my husband was alive.' 'My friends used to ask me to tea, but they made sure I was gone before their husbands came home.' There is a general, but unhappy acceptance: 'You're only asked to lunch, never dinner.'

It isn't just a limit placed on their social scene. 'People – even family – take advantage of you when you have no husband to stand up for you.' 'There was this natural assumption, now I'm alone, I'd be at their beck and call.' Harder yet can be the rejection from one's children: 'Within a few weeks of his father's death, my son said to me I would have to get on a bus or something. This was obviously to convey that they (he had a wife who may have been fearful of her mother-in-law's intrusion on their life) wouldn't take me home. I was too overwhelmed to say anything.' In fairness, perhaps her son may have been trying to make his mother face reality – albeit too fast.

It is now that the widow realizes just how much adult social life is conducted in pairs. 'Lots of people drop widows from their social round.' 'A neighbour once said she would invite me to her dinner party, if she could find a partner; otherwise, I couldn't come – it would upset her table arrangements.' In this particular case the friendship did not end, the widow accepted that such tactless behaviour would be part of her lot.

The younger the widow, the worse it can be: 'Overnight, my status had changed. People still don't know how to treat me. I don't fit into the usual category of widow.' This young woman had discovered that the public still pictures a widow as elderly. 'At times, I feel almost contagious. If the central heating packs up or the roof falls in, male neighbours and friends' husbands don't want to come over and help a young widow.' In their defence, it could be that they assume that as one of the new, independent female generation, she can do it for herself!

Well-known and wealthy widows suffer a similar shrinkage in their social circle: 'To be honest, there is a disappointment when you see how some friendships change just because Lyndon has gone' – Mrs L. B. Johnson.

Rejection can cause a lot of depression and additional despair: 'I longed for someone to ask me in for coffee. People had said, just come in, but somehow, I couldn't make the first move.' 'I was longing for some companionship – a friend with whom I could go to the theatre or dinner – but women I met at a social club were only interested in men and I wasn't ready for that yet.'

Drugs of one kind or another are all too frequently seen as the answer to what outsiders feel is a 'widow's winge'. One can understand sleeping pills, because it is with great difficulty most widows go alone to the bed they shared with their man. Tranquillizers, on the other hand, only stave off the moment of reality. Sooner or later, it has to be faced.

Evelyn le Chêne, journalist, lecturer and specialist in military affairs, had married a man who was many years her senior. They had moved to France when his health deteriorated. She took a crash course in nursing in order to be able to feed him oxygen, give him injections and drips. All this medical paraphernalia was most distressing to face when she returned from the hospital in Lyons where he died. She went back to England and withdrew from the public eye for the first two years. 'I couldn't write and tell anyone. I couldn't bring myself to put down the words that said, Pierre was dead. I disappeared – went to ground – refused all pills and potions – Pierre was against drugs.' Pierre had suffered the horrors of a concentration camp during the Second World War and yet, or perhaps because of that, his advice had always been 'Take a deep breath and go through it without those drugs.'

Katie Boyle also advocates managing without drugs, which are, in reality, a crutch more than a medication. 'I think to have been drugged on that day (the funeral) would have been most insulting. I owed it to him.'

A strong sense of duty is what makes women like this 'tough it out'. Not everyone has such strength. The danger needs to be brought home to them before they see the foolishness of their actions: 'I was one year on valium, then crossed the road without looking out for traffic. I had been walking like a zombie. A driver went for me: "Don't commit suicide in front of my car." I was jolted out of taking the pills.'

Jane had fallen into a deep depression. She had not only discovered that her husband had kept his age from her (he was thirty years her senior), but she was snowed under by a huge pile of his unpaid bills. Foolishly, she accepted the pills that were pressed on her. Even more dangerous was the fact they came from someone unqualified. 'I was not in control of myself and they were turning me into a lunatic, making me suicidal.' With the best of intentions, her mother conned her into going into a mental clinic. She told her it was to see a back doctor (she suffers from back trouble). As soon as Jane realized the truth about the place she got out of there, and, most importantly, stopped taking the pills.

The sense of aloneness which assaults widows, the lack of a husband who 'cares', can send them into such a deep depression that only medical attention will be able to pull them free. Depression was what finally ushered Betty into a mental home, unconscious of the fact she was even there. When she came to, a doctor was sitting at her side. 'I thought he had been there all night and it gave me an extraordinary feeling of support.' Once she was in that home, she was out of her self-imposed isolation. The doctor finally persuaded her to come out of her room and into the lounge of the home. 'When I sat looking out over the beautiful gardens, the mental pain was lessened.'

However forward-looking the older generation of women can be in their attitudes towards having a career and an identity of their own, they often still retain prejudices of the past, when it was considered: 'You take your position from your husband when you marry and are not really anyone in your own right.' Even Eleanor Roosevelt, who had her own public following, told a newspaper a few days after her husband's death: 'The story is over, they will forget me now.' She confessed to a friend: 'I feel very inadequate.'

This feeling of inadequacy and helplessness can and does go on. Yoko Ono admits that she has felt bewildered for four years. The passing of time can make it worse, not better. Eleven years after Winston Churchill's death, Clementine wrote to her daughter. 'I do miss Papa so, really more than I did just after he died.' Nor has Bette Hill found time to be a great healer: 'It isn't, and the more time goes by the more I miss Graham.'

Twenty years on, one lady carried her husband's picture everywhere she went, whether in hotel or hospital, because she continued to feel the need to have 'my Sammy to talk to'. A lifetime later, Florence, a First World War widow, will tell you, she has a wonderful home, a kind daughter and son-in-law, grandchildren and great-grandchildren. Who can ask for more? She can; because there was 'only one gentleman in my life.' It would appear that Picasso's widow could not face up to the exhibition she had prepared to celebrate the 105th anniversary of his birth. A few days before, in the autumn of 1986, she took her own life.

'When there are dark patches, I remember Jack Buchanan singing "There's always tomorrow to give us a smile,"' said Anna Neagle, who was widowed in 1977. She kept that smiling face in place for her public. What she felt in private was never revealed. The majority will eventually come to terms with reality. 'I still think of my husband a lot. You can't help it really', said the woman whose husband died in his line of duty. 'I go through periods of bitterness, but then I look at the starving in Ethiopia and the international tragedies and I start to get it in perspective.'

An equally sensible summing up of the situation is shown in this extract of a letter written by an Israeli war widow, thanking her London hosts for their kindness to her on holiday in the summer of 1986:

'When you lose someone very dear to you, you lose with him many things: the confidence and expectations of life, the ability to give and take; something in you dies together with him. The suddenness, the unexpected death and finality, about which you cannot do anything, leaves you helpless and frustrated.

'At such moments you discover that the will to live is stronger than your very self and stronger than anything you feel, and thus you survive. Mere survival, however, is no life. You can only live with the cooperation of others. Everyone does it in their own way, but no one can do it alone. You do it with the help of family, friends, and caring people who open their hearts and homes for you with such warmth. When your child asks you, "Why are we such a small family – only you and me?" then, wholeheartedly, I can now tell him: "We have a large warm family"; and because I believe it, he does. Thank you for everything.'

5

Something to hold on to

'I remember being glad we were both in the same Southern Hemisphere and looking at the same stars'
– Catherine

The writer on the previous page had reached the time to take stock of her situation; the time to draw deep breath; to think of positive things instead of running away from the negative ones. To look for and find, however tiny the shred of satisfaction, it can be there, even though he is not. 'Two weeks before he died, while spending the weekend on the boat, he told me he now felt he had everything he wanted.' It is a compliment to cling to even though the Captain is not there.

Katie Boyle says: 'I remember thinking after he died, Oh, thank God I have said all the things I wanted to.' She, like other widows, decided to stay put in the home she had shared with her husband, at least for a while: 'I wanted to see four seasons go by.' The garden can provide a link between the widow's life and the man's death. He may not see the flowers bloom, but at least he planted them. They are still something that can be shared. The grandchildren who arrive later can be seen as 'his stake in the future', however difficult it may be to see them cuddled in his favourite chair, reading his books or splashing in the swimming pool. A widow from Essex remembers: 'At first it was hard. He used to come in from work and go out and swim up and down while I prepared dinner. Now, when I see the grandchildren out there, they are sharing one of his pleasures. I know he would be pleased.'

One woman has managed to draw such a vivid verbal picture of that un-met grandfather to his grandson, the boy talks about him like an old friend: 'He even knows his likes and dislikes.' She can enjoy a conversation with him that would bore anyone else.

There is a reason why many women are reluctant to move or part with what was his. They can keep to the pattern of the life they shared. This can outweigh the pain. Catherine still has Chris's car bright and shining in the garage.

Sarah has made one minor change in her house. She has moved his favourite chair, which was at the front window: 'When he could no longer go out, he used to sit there and watch for my return when I went shopping. I was always so glad to see the top of his white head as I came round the corner.' Now that chair sits in the place where she spends most of her time, in the conservatory: 'I always wanted this to become an extension of our living room, but he never did and I didn't like to nag.' Nor will she now consider any such structural change. All she has done is put a new cover on the worn seat of that chair.

There is an equal closeness with the family pet: 'He absorbed all the tears'; 'having a dog to come home to was a great help.' It is a tie few would want to break. 'We had our dog and two puppies in the car with us,' says Pamela. 'Only one survived. He was found running around in a field by a farmer near the scene of the accident. The farmer came to the hospital to tell my son he would take care of it until he could. I wanted to let him keep it but my son said that was all we had left. My plans were to go to England as soon as I was fit enough to travel; the US Navy were shipping all my household goods over. I knew the puppy would have to go into quarantine, but we still went ahead and did it and I'm glad. We've had a member of that puppy's family ever since.'

One of Eleanor Roosevelt's first acts on leaving the White House was to retrieve their dog, who had been staying with friends during the arrangements which led up to the funeral.

The advantage of pets is that they need someone to care for them. A woman does not feel so completely alone if she has a pet, a 'someone' for whom there is still a need to shop, 'someone' still relying on her. Anna Neagle had 'two very important cats'; Dorothy Lamour eventually gave in to her sons' insistence she have a dog and discovered: 'I wasn't moping as much'. One woman is so devoted to her dog, 'he even goes to church with me'.

The question of what to do with the husband's clothes proves difficult. Those who feel that removing them from the house will remove the sorrow should think again. It is better to ignore them for a while. At one time, Hilda considered storing the contents of her husband's wardrobe: 'But I can't; I had even thought to ask my girls to do it for me, and let me leave while it was being done, but I am not going to do that.'

She is wise, because those who give them away too fast regret it later. They were treasures they would have preferred to keep. They had lost the extra comfort of bridging a bad gap clothed in the sweater or some other piece of attire he favoured: 'Whenever I went "down", I pulled on one of his jumpers'; 'I wore his scarves in the coldest weather and it made me feel much better.' A lady who delayed for two years on her decision, eventually gave everything away but his ties: 'He loved them too much. I'd have burned them before I'd have done that.'

A war widow had to wait forty-two years for a remembrance. Then, to her great joy, a teenager in Holland uncovered the remains of the bomber in which her husband had been shot down. He found a gold cuff link in the débris: 'It's wonderful to have something like this to remember Joe by, I somehow feel more at peace now.'

Evelyn has kept all her husband's medals and uniforms, even though they belong to a time before she knew him. It was the book she was to write about Mauthausen, where he had been imprisoned, that had brought them together. Despite his name, Pierre was a British Intelligence Officer who had served as an agent. 'Every time I open the wardrobe, he's there.'

Daphne du Maurier writes in her book how 'to ease the pain, I took over some of his things, wore his shirts, sat at his writing desk, used his pens to acknowledge the hundreds of letters of condolence and by the very process of identification, with the objects he had touched, felt closer to him.'

Cynthia found her solace in a verse from the Bible: 'Anytime I felt the least bit lost, I read it, I kept a copy in my wallet. "And God shall wipe away all tears from their eyes and there shall be no more death, neither sorrow nor crying, neither shall be any more pain for the former things are passed away".'

Quite naturally, the letters of condolence assume a great importance as well as providing comfort: 'I clung to them. They kept me close to him', Lauren Bacall said. She also planned to assemble all the newspaper clippings into an album for her children. Vicky has all the cuttings about her husband's loss at sea in an impressive album with the last photographs taken by the shipmate who survived. 'It was six months before he could bring himself to give them to me.'

Frances Anne has her husband's watch, which was to be the catalyst in bringing her back to reality. She had sent a crucifix to the Island priest to be placed on his grave. He sent back a photograph of what he had done: 'I stared at it. How could this possibly be my husband buried there? I looked at the watch I was wearing – it was his – and finally accepted what had happened.'

Some women feel for a long time that the man's spirit is dominating the house, and are glad: 'He's here, I feel him with me.' Barbara felt very strongly that way because: 'He was so determined not to let go when I drove him to the hospital. After he died I felt he was still there. Friends who came to call said the same.' She sought an explanation from a spiritualist, who said: 'When a person dies suddenly, they go through a traumatic experience. They are wrenched very roughly soul from body. They need time to really go.'

Others may prefer to apply logic in cases like this. One must accept that everyone is taken by surprise, and they are unable to absorb the shock of his departure that fast. They are searching for him, so certain he is still in his favourite chair, he *will* be there when they look. It can make them reluctant to move from the house. In Barbara's case, while she began to recognize that a smaller house would make more sense: 'I wanted the house we had to go to someone special.' Then Derek Jacobi, who had starred in *I, Claudius* which her husband had scripted, was house-hunting. He made her an offer she did not want to refuse: 'It was as if it was staying in the family.'

There can be an equal attachment to the place where a husband died. For several years, Mary Hemingway gathered friends round her in the hunting lodge to celebrate 'Papa's birthday'. Bette Hill had bulbs planted near the scarred tree where his plane crashed: 'And when I'm feeling low and want to be near Graham, I go over to that copse and feel so close to him there.'

Kathleen Kennedy had to go over to Belgium to the place where her husband had died and was now buried. Catherine, whose husband died in the Falklands, feels that visiting there was a milestone down her path of widowhood. A widow of an earlier war agrees: 'I did not feel the reality of my husband's death until I walked the Normandy beaches.' This need has finally been officially recognized, and the British Legion have arranged visits for widows to distant battlegrounds and cemeteries. Who can forget the poignant picture of one of them weeping across the stone of a military cemetery in the Far East?

Many of the women who gather yearly in Whitehall on the day before the Official Service of Remembrance only have the Cenotaph on which to place their flowers. So truly was their man lost in some foreign field or distant sea, it is their sole marker of his death. They have no local cemetery, no gravestone where they can sit and talk to him. It makes their loss even more difficult to bear. They have to find something else to cling to. Some find it in the medals that were awarded later. One can see the proud sparkle on their coats as they march up to the Cenotaph for the service, but one can also see the bitter tears of some who prefer to stay on the sidelines. Perhaps the political figures who squabble over their order of precedence attend on the wrong day! Those women left behind to soldier on alone are as significant as the poppy-topped crosses planted in front of Westminster Abbey.

Religion can prove a great comfort: 'I believe my faith gave me strength and courage'; 'I have my talks with God now and again'. 'I cried so much at first, I felt obliged to leave the church, but the Deacon followed me and helped me through the Communion Services,' says Marie of her first visit. 'I spent every Sunday crying, but it got less and less as time went by – finally I could go for several weeks without even a tear. I suppose I was returning to my roots – I went to Sunday School and Church about three or four times a week when I was very young.'

A lady of another faith recounted how: 'I felt the need to go to a service, but not at our usual place of worship. There, I had this strange and wonderful feeling like arms were enclosing me. The minister said I had had a religious experience.'

A clairvoyant would have said otherwise. They can play an important part in many widows' lives, as they link them to their husbands. Katie is strongly in their favour: 'I believed in life after death before Greville died, but have so many proofs now. I went to a medium after a message from him was passed through the mother of a friend.'

Someone else summoned in a similar way was visiting with a relative when 'the clairvoyant exclaimed, "It's coming through for you." I established a closeness with my husband.' It pulled her out of a terrible depression. She finds a six-monthly visit very supportive. 'We have a talk and it is all very reassuring.'

Kim Casali of the 'Love is . . .' cartoon fame also has

recourse to clairvoyants. She had known her husband's case was terminal, but they had played the usual 'of course you'll get better' game. This meant she could not question him about the business which he had managed as it had expanded. The cartoon was now emblazoned on all manner of items worldwide. Alone, she had all kinds of worries to do with distribution – should she let someone else take over? She turned to a clairvoyant to reach him: 'Ninety per cent of what she told me has worked out. My husband came through, it had to be him – everything he told me meant something. He had messages for the children and everything.' She feels this has now given a new meaning to her life: 'Now, I know he is there and I know he is watching and looking after us.'

The only widow who did not seem to benefit from a clairvoyant was the one who had been married to the heir to the Winchester rifle fortune. She was told that she was haunted by the ghosts of all the victims of those rifles, and spent the next thirty-eight years building a mansion in California where doorways led to blank walls. Her other efforts to confuse the ghosts led to staircases going nowhere, and the mansion ended up with one hundred and sixty rooms and two thousand doors.

Nearly every widow would like to do something 'special' in her husband's memory. Few can achieve the grand memorial that Queen Victoria put up for her beloved Albert in Kensington Gardens. There have been some other impressive gestures. The Begum Aga Khan has a grand mausoleum facing their summer villa. A single rose is placed there daily. Baroness Rothschild has offered Jerusalem a new National Supreme Court. Celia Lipton has donated a million dollars to the hospital where her husband died. Mary Hemingway had founded an Ernest Hemingway Prize for fiction, ten years before she died.

Memorials which come from admirers are no less appreciated. Eleanor Roosevelt was invited to unveil the statue of Franklin D. Roosevelt which a British subscription raised in Grosvenor Square, London. There is a Performing Arts

Center and an airport in John Kennedy's name. Baroness Churchill could turn in several directions, from Churchill College Cambridge, to statues in Parliament Square, Essex and Kent. Bette opened a school in Graham Hill's name in Italy. Many other examples could be given.

In a more individualistic manner, Barbara Cartland's car licence plate is: 'Twenty-nine, his favourite number when he played roulette'. Sally Oppenheimer had her old name hyphenated on to the new when she married again. Susan Crosland, who had written professionally as Susan Barnes during her marriage, took on 'the one I loved best' after he died. Beryl Maudling, widow of the one time Tory Chancellor, donated her two thousand condolence letters from round the world to the archives of Churchill College. Marina sent hers to Stanford University, along with Lord Vaizey's papers. 'The Hoover Institute there expressed an interest in them to add to their collection of papers on Domestic and International affairs relating to the politics, economics and social history of the 20th Century.' These were subjects in which Lord Vaizey was involved. She later received an unexpected and pleasant surprise when the leading physiotherapy training centre in the UK at Wakefield Yorkshire notified her they planned to name the new wing after him. 'He had taken a lot of interest in their work.'

On a lesser scale, but one as important to Joan C., she donated a kennel in Denis's name to the Canine Defence League, because 'he loved dogs'. She is also very involved in a photographic exhibition for ex-servicemen in Richmond which was another of his interests. Many widows have made donations to the hospitals which they felt kept their husbands alive, however much they may have felt in retrospect it was on 'borrowed time'. Pamela searched for and found some of the original books on the Methodist religion (to which her husband subscribed). These were donated in his name to a library of religious books at Chatanooga, Tennessee, the nearest town to the place of his death.

Widows of entertainers can forever keep company on film with the man they married. Sue Ladd is able constantly to screen her hero, who came into her office when she was an agent: 'He looked like a young Greek god and was unforgettable'. He will forever be able to stay that way for her. Freddie, widow of Tony Hancock, says: 'I am very lucky, as my husband is as alive as ever in the eyes of the people.' Many famous singers' widows are surrounded by their songs. Mrs Matt Munro's condition of sale of their house was that a collection of his records stay behind: 'I want his music to go on in the house.'

A lot of women write about their men, not just biographies. They can fly to his defence. When a prominent newspaper columnist in the USA began a series of covert attacks on her, Eleanor Roosevelt knew they were really aimed at the President. She dealt with the detractor firmly; 'Franklin achieved too much of great importance to be blurred by malice.'

Lady Oswald Mosley's reasons seem to be protective: 'I think one has a duty to put the record right if one can. It is very irritating when people go on telling the same old lies.' Even if one does not agree with her opinions, one has to understand her loyalty.

Some seek to go into battle on their man's behalf with the spoken word. Madame Ngo Dinh Nhu, who narrowly escaped the knifing which killed her husband and his brother, the President of Vietnam, is a prime example. She embarked on a lecture tour of the United States pouring out such fiery condemnation of President Kennedy for what she saw as his responsibility for what happened, that the Press nicknamed her Dragon Lady. She had vanished from the public stage by the time the United States became heavily embroiled in her country's war, so her further comments went unrecorded.

It was with great satisfaction that Evelyn heard Klaus Barbie had been found. He was her husband's principal tormentor in Mauthausen concentration camp. She will be one of the few journalists allowed into his trial, but may have a long wait. There seems to be a constant delay.

One woman has been fighting for her husband's good name for more than forty years to correct the records of the War Office. 'I want his name cleared. He was never a deserter; Paddy loved the Army.' Two men who read her most recent plea in a newspaper came forward as witnesses and now he has been officially declared the hero he was. His name has been added to the Roll of Honour: 'It's fantastic,' she says.

Widows have been moved to write poetry about their lives with their husbands. Most of these books are published privately, which is a pity because they would provide solace for those who think in a similar way, even if they cannot express themselves so well.

There are many who will not rest easy until they have completed plans made together. 'In that last year or two, we had built a villa in the South of France. The Easter before he died, we went out and furnished it. We were to return on 6th June. He died on the 1st. The first visit there, I sat in the garden and cried.' In the end, this widow found it easier to sell the memories. She then decided to take some of the trips they had planned. 'I was very sad on the way to the Taj Mahal, but determined to do it. The beauty of the building kept me happy once I arrived.'

Marie was another determined to go ahead with what had been planned. She went on the photo safari which should have celebrated their Silver Wedding: 'And I enjoyed it.' In many ways, keeping to those last plans made is a symbolic gesture.

6

Guilts, regrets, memories

'Beware of the "if onlys"'

This is a time of mixed emotions, when the photographs which have been hidden away or turned down are back in place, or more often now take pride of place. Then, to their dismay, women may find a feeling of hatred infiltrating itself into the sorrow they feel for their husband. This leaves them bewildered. However, the intensity of that hate, which is usually brief, is part of the normal bereavement process. In most cases, the anger is there because they feel that 'he' has allowed himself to be lured away from them, by death.

This agitation begins to encompass memories of their married life. Finally they arrive at guilt, a feeling which cannot easily be discarded. For many, their guilt can be as trivial as: 'I never made him the milk puddings I knew he loved.' While from there, they may go on to remember that unfinished quarrel, the boat she stopped him buying, the holiday postponed until now when it is too late. None are serious enough complaint for a living marriage; but, oh, the damage they can do after death! Too many widows pile unnecessary blame on themselves. As one lady admitted: 'I still have a longing to be punished.' It is self-flagellation – a need to suffer – part of their guilt is in being alive while he is dead.

Kathleen Kennedy was in a terrible state. Her sister-in-law

reported: 'I never met anyone so desperately unhappy. She regretted she had not become pregnant and said: "Well, I guess God has taken care of the matter in His own way, hasn't He?"' When the war ended in 1945, she went on a succession of religious retreats to a nunnery in Kendal. She hoped to re-enter the church after her excommunication by marriage.

Betty had found that: 'The first five months were a doddle. I almost wondered if I had loved him.' However, a time bomb of trouble began ticking away as she looked back on her marriage. 'It was as if the Devil had recorded every failure. I was pretty bloody, I grumbled a lot.' Boredom had been the culprit. She had found the switch from a busy business life in town to the domesticity of suburbia difficult to endure. To keep her happy, they had moved – twice – each move causing problems of finance, adjustment, and extra travel for him.

As Betty worked her way back over this thorny ground, she heard that stress could cause cancer. She snatched at that label of blame and pinned it on her complaining self. This sent her into a terrible decline. She took to her bed, a supply of Sonoral close to hand; promising herself that, once her son by her first marriage was through with college, 'I had a date with those pills.' Rebuffing all the concerned calls from friends, she deteriorated rapidly until she was: 'filthy, unwashed and suffering extraordinary mental pain.' Luckily, one friend refused to be put off and barged in with a doctor: 'I was quite potty by then and told him I had killed my husband.'

This situation of a wife blaming herself for the husband's death is quite a common occurrence. 'I felt I had been too tough on him,' said another. 'If I hadn't been so difficult, he wouldn't have gone to live abroad (which was where he was killed in a car crash). I felt he would have been better for the children if I had died. I felt responsible for his death.'

Equally, if a husband has been ill prior to his death, he leaves behind a lot of reasons for the widow to reproach herself unnecessarily: 'I felt guilty because I did not stay at the hospital at night.' Hilda chose to forget she had spent every other available minute with him. One may understand those who say 'I found it hard to watch him suffer', but to feel guilty because 'I didn't do enough, I could have been more patient', is an extra twist of the knife. Worse yet are those who feel they could or should have saved him. 'We had pulled him through that dangerous illness when we were on holiday,' says Joan C. 'I felt I'd used up all my prayers there.'

'Did I do everything I could have done?' Too many women belabour themselves with this question. Joan Morecambe admits she was left with such a lingering doubt. Could she have called the surgeon who operated on Eric when he was taken ill that last time? 'If I'd rung Harefield, someone would have bleeped him. I'm not saying that Magdi (the famous heart specialist) could have worked wonders, but I wish I'd thought of asking him.' Every widow who ever rushed her husband to hospital wishes that she could have thought of everything. But there is no rehearsal for this event. Too many take too long before they can accept that nothing else they could have done would have made any difference. Fortunately, Joan Morecambe had a friend who cautioned: 'Beware of the "if onlys"', and she put the whole situation into perspective.

Marjory worried: 'Why didn't I fuss over him more?' It did no good at that time to be reminded he had been the sort of man who didn't like her to fuss. That was no longer important. 'I felt terrible that, instead of saying comforting things to him while he was in hospital, I acted flippant, as I had always been, because he preferred me to be that way.' This guilt was what sent her in hiding from her family for a while.

Madame El Said began to ask herself why she had insisted on leaving Iraq to study for her doctorate in economics. 'Then, I saw it as a blessing.' This was a far more realistic view, since her move had at least brought her sons to safety. If they had stayed they would have been likely to have also perished from the assassins' bullets.

Will the widow of the man who set off a chaos of killing in a restaurant in California be left for ever regretting she did not check to see if he had made an appointment with a mental clinic? If so, it would be as well to remember, even if she had, that there was no guarantee he would have kept it. Better to feel that in death he freed her and their children from his stress.

Do any of the women who were provoked into inducing their widowhood by their own hand feel worse or better for what they have done? Unfortunately, none were willing to be interviewed. But those who were fiendishly battered, either physically or mentally before taking that last resort, can only induce sympathy. One hopes they will accept the verdicts that cleared them and get on with their lives.

Most difficult to look back on seems to be suicide, especially if there were previous attempts. Should they have recognized a cry for help? When it finally happens, a widow can be left with self-recrimination which will retard her recovery. Cynthia suffered badly in this fashion. She spent a lot of time walking along the Atlantic shore near her mother's home trying to reason why. In the hope of some answers, she studied the history of suicide: 'I discovered that in the past, in early times, suicides had been buried at the crossroads or outside church walls. The most celebrated suicide was Plato, and hara kiri was a method of death honoured by the Japanese.' None of this stopped her blaming herself. 'I shouldn't have taken that degree.' She forgot that the reason was to improve her own capabilities and to help them out of their dismal financial situation. She had, in fact, crammed two years' work into one. This may have been why she was not aware of his worsening condition.

In the hope of working her way through her feelings of guilt she went to see a minister. Unfortunately, instead of dealing with her spiritual needs, he chose to try to administer some physical comfort. This is just one of the several despicable acts perpetrated on widows in need that were related to the writer.

When such widows agonize over 'why?', they should try to remember that when a man decides to kill himself the balance of his mind is disturbed, so no matter in how exemplary a fashion a wife behaves she still cannot sway a totally irrational mind. He was not the man who was her husband. Some suffer a sense of betrayal that can turn to the bitterness such as one woman experienced when she felt her husband had chosen this way out of their turmoil-filled life, plagued by impossibly behaved children. 'You bastard, you've left me with them,' she had screamed into his carbon-monoxide-filled car.

'It was him who wanted to move away,' said one who is now cut off from friends and family. He had chosen to retire to a new bungalow on the coast. That was where he hanged himself: 'They seem to feel it is my fault,' she said of those who had deserted her. And Freddie Hancock still shudders at the memory of feeling 'every person staring at me because Tony died.'

Such women cannot rid themselves of the feeling that there was 'more' they could have done. This is probably not so. A man determined to end it all will finally find a way. One woman was very practical. 'I had lived through three years of hell; when it finally happened, total peace descended on me. By his death, he gave me freedom and a chance of a second life.'

This same sensible attitude should be exercised at the conclusion of the game of 'Of course you'll get better,' that so many couples are forced to play in the last days of a terminal illness. It would be more rewarding to look back after and tell oneself: 'having kept him happy, I had achieved something.' It took Betty some time to remember that in his diary her husband had written of the last one they spent together: 'Best Christmas ever'. Or, as Joan R. said of those extra six months her husband fought for: 'It was the happiest time of our lives.'

They are then not as likely to be left with regrets, like Mrs L. B. Johnson, who says: 'One should live every day to the fullest, as though you had a short supply; because that is what you have. I said that glibly for years, but I didn't know how intensely one should live.' She adds: 'There are so many things I wish I'd done. But I put my thoughts into two categories; the "aren't you glad thats" and the "if onlys". I try to keep the second column as short as possible. We should think of the first column ahead of time and savour things when we have them. To be close to death gives you a new awareness of the preciousness of life and the extreme tenuousness of it.' She knows that 'people expect to find me enveloped in sadness, but I am not. Lyndon goes on living in so much I think and do. I pick up my evening bag and there is his cigar left over from an evening we had together. He would always ask me to carry his cigars so they wouldn't crush in the pocket of his suit. I come upon these things and I feel a pang, but I also feel warm and comforted.'

Quite a few of the women interviewed were mired down in unhappy marriages from which they did not have the courage to pull free. They clung to the vow 'for better or worse', and then found lonely widowhood worse yet. In addition, a few interviewees admitted that all was not as they might have liked in their marriage, even to quarrels on the very morning their husband died. However, in deference to the tradition that 'one should speak no ill of the dead', they did not wish to elaborate. For them, it was preferable to prop up the crumbled marriage with the frame: 'They were so happy'.

A small number made honest admissions on those miserable marriages: one so basic as to be a rejoicing on the news of the death: 'I'm free'. One said she had pronounced: 'Good riddance' as the ambulance carried him off, and that she had refused to go to the funeral because 'enough was enough'. A woman who ended up identifying her husband's body in Skid Row said: 'I felt no pity for him, he had put me through hell.' Another: 'He'd made my life a misery, forbidding me to go out, and if I stood up to him he would make a scene outside the house.' However, in this particular situation, this lady's conscience would not allow her to desert him when he was ill. She nursed him for three years. Her widowhood came as a great relief. She has no worries about the future because 'I had had thirty-four years to cope with most situations.'

Freedom from marriage has many connotations. Some

women are now free from the stress of worrying over a terminally ill husband. They can go off on an escapade of spending, travel or any other indulgence, without that worried look over the shoulder for the invalid in bed. Several, freed from what they felt was an unhappy marriage, may find to some surprise that they want to search through the débris for a few pieces of pleasure they can shine up to make it look better than it was, or: 'I miss the blighter more than I thought I ever would!' Those who suffered physical damage will no longer have to hide the results. They will finally see their bruises fade.

For others, it will be as simple as being free to do what they wanted, instead of always deferring to their men's wishes. They may not have been unhappy in that state, but feel they have a lot of living to do of their own choice. They have been known to bounce across deserts in Land Rovers at an advanced age, scale mountains in helicopters or take flying lessons in their mid-seventies.

The one who trained to be a glider pilot said: 'My husband always hated the idea of flying.' So she had to wait. Now she has chalked up many solo flights, and feels: 'As long as you have your health, there's nothing you can't achieve.'

As important is the return to what they gave up for marriage: 'My career was a problem,' says Marguerite Wolff, who was on the crest of her career as a concert pianist when she met her husband. 'He was very proud of my playing to start with, but gradually he wanted me for himself.' To appease him, she stopped playing in public and concentrated on being a wife, then a mother to their two daughters. She missed the career for which she had been trained: 'I felt I was not using myself enough.' When her husband died, the visitor who came with more than a condolence call was Louis Kentner. 'He told me he had arranged a programme for me; I went back to work.' This has not precluded her from mourning, but when depression hits Marguerite, she has no need for drugs. 'I just sit down and practise on the piano.'

She can now do exactly what she wants without hurting

anyone's feelings. Both her daughters are grown up and have their own lives. 'I can practise as much as I want, usually eight hours a day; I don't have to explain to anyone. I do these huge tours (she travels worldwide) – you cannot tour successfully if you are married.'

Her first professional concert in widowhood was at Shrewsbury: 'I arrived at the station, and there was that old familiar feeling. An arrival of an artist is different to that of anyone else. I said to myself: "I have come home"'.

Celia had already cut one album: 'The Big Band and Broadcasting Sound', before her husband died. 'Victor was pleased, but asked: "Are you going anywhere?" For him, one had to aim for success.' At that time, her response had been that it was 'her thing – like his boat'. 'I wasn't going to mess up my marriage.' Now Celia is pursuing a return to her career with all the ambition he would have wished. 'I knew there was no reason for me to sit in a rocking chair staring at the palm trees or getting drunk with the broads all day.'

Jane Withers had been a child star, the spoiled brat of the 1930s movies. She had collected thousands of dolls from fans in those days. 'My husband never liked those dolls.' Now she can do what she wants without any interference. They are on display in a studio she has built to produce films in her own right.

Ann Monserrat had travelled with her husband, the famous writer, from islands as distant from each other as the St Lawrence Seaway from the Mediterranean. She has now chosen to settle permanently on the one she liked best – Gozo – and is doing some writing herself.

Other women are ready to pick up their freedom and GO. The places their husbands did not want to visit are waiting for them. There is nothing to stop their take-off. 'You can do it – if you try.' And if you want to! It might be the first time in their lives they have discovered this. It can put confidence back in their hands or make them realize their capabilities: 'I depended so very much on my husband and our marriage. It never occurred to me that I might be able to do things on my own. Since I have been widowed, I find I can drive my car to the South of France and know my way about in entertaining. The children are astonished at me.' Which proves that if 'Pussy wants to come off that silken cushion' on which she has happily sat for years, she slides off with a great deal of satisfaction.

What of the women who discover that death has parted the curtains round their husband's secret life? As it unravels before them, how do they deal with this married lie they had been living? Some women have been known to take that unexpected illegitimate child into the fold of the family. Does one accept or reject the mistress who wishes to come to the funeral? The women have been known to grieve together. Queen Alexandra had even invited Mrs Keppel to share the bedside death watch for her husband, King Edward VII.

Mrs Eleanor Roosevelt chose to keep her cool public image when she discovered that the woman she had thought banished from the President's life had been at his death bed. She herself had been instructed to carry on as usual so as not to scare the public. When she discovered a portrait of him which she knew nothing about, she guessed it had been commissioned by the 'other woman'. One has to admire her dignity in sending it to her. Jackie Kennedy chose the 'no comment' way out as scandal erupted around her husband's name. As the book goes to press, the widow of the assassinated Swedish Premier, Olof Palme, has also chosen to keep her silence. Mrs Tommy Cooper fended off her husband's voluble lady friend with her own story to the Press, other widows are glad to 'tell all' when it comes to their own autobiographies.

Women who as innocent brides found they had married a homosexual or a transvestite have been known to continue to cover the tragic farce of their marriages, even after the death. It is a brave woman who can admit to the world that she has been so foolishly misled. Nor does every widow wish to make a scene if misleading obituaries are published. Lady Stanley Baker chose to make no further comment on Richard Burton's rambling anecdotes which bore little resemblance to the husband she knew.

Under such circumstances, a dignified silence is the best possible answer to keeping the memory of their man from being tarnished.

7

Single parenting and sexual problems

'I told the children straight: "Your father's dead"'

Death is no respecter of age. While the glowing bride walking out of the church hand-in-hand with her husband may not consider herself vulnerable, death can already be snapping at the heels of the groom.

There would be a fierce debate if one were to suggest which category of widow suffers the most. But widowhood visited upon a young woman undoubtedly presents extra problems. 'The anger was really the worse, because I expected I'd always have a husband to be there and help with the kids.' Never again will they hear the call – 'Daddy's home!' On a totally practical plane: 'With four young children, even going out to post a letter was quite a performance.'

Usually, she is not yet conditioned to anything but happiness. The bloom of the early years of marriage promises a rainbow-coloured future. Up to the moment that sniper killed her husband, nothing bad had happened in Frances Anne's life. She was a petted, only daughter, who grew up to marry her sweetheart. Their happiness was completed with a baby who was ten weeks old when his father died. She was to find, as have others in her position, that the baby was the anchor with which she steadied herself. 'I'm sure having the baby was the one thing that kept me sane. I felt he was my prime responsibility and, fortunately, he needed my attention twenty-four hours a day'. 'Initially, I lived from day to day, concentrating all my energies on my son'; 'I just couldn't jump out of the window, which I might otherwise have done', said a former Miss World, pregnant with the child she and her husband had waited for through several years of marriage.

It may be that statistics prove young mothers have a suicidal tendency in this situation. However, the doctor who came to tell Louise that her husband was dead brought two nuns with him, not to comfort her but 'to stand by the window in case I jumped out, when all I wanted to do was get home to the baby.'

There is no training for the role of young widowed mother. 'The children didn't just lose their father, they lost their happy mother,' says a woman whose day had started normally with her husband going to work and ended with him dead. From then on, she was always aware of her position as the only parent: 'The children's needs came first.'

It can make a mother highly resourceful and in some cases force her to take a chance, because she has no other choice. Joan R., waiting to get out of India, was faced with a quandary as their names came to the top of the shipping list. Her youngest child – no more than a baby – came down with pneumonia. He was unfit to travel. What should she now do? Her solution was in one of the condolence letters which had offered: 'Anything I can do to help, I will.' She sent this friend of her husband's a cable: 'Please take delivery of two small boys,' and packed them off on the next ship. Then she devoted herself to getting the baby well as quickly as possible.

The dual roles played by father and mother now become her sole responsibility. 'And it is a hell of a responsibility. I am the stick in the middle of the Maypole, and they need me', said Bette Hill of those years when her children were growing up. One mother saw her husband's sudden death as the cause of her children maturing overnight. 'I just can't put my finger on it, but they seem more worldly-wise.'

Another said: 'I missed him most and still miss him most in

relation to the children, their successes and triumphs, their problems and tragedies.' Troubles should be shared between father and mother.

Kim Casali added to her responsibilities when she chose to have her third child posthumously. It was the one important discussion she was able to have with her husband when he was ill. 'He knew I wanted a larger family and agreed to this arrangement.' In spite of the fragility of his health he was able to be the donor. She does not see any difference in her sons and is now often called upon to comment or give advice to widows in similar situations. The most recent instance was when a French woman was suing the hospital for the return of her dead husband's sperm.

Children of school age have additional and different problems. Mothers deep in their own grief sometimes forget that they are also suffering: 'I handled it badly. I was pining for my husband, my son was pining for the father he idolized'; 'I underestimated the effect it had on the children. They took it hard, though I didn't realize it at the time'; 'My son never got over the fact that he had not been at his father's funeral. I thought he would be better off staying on at boarding school'; 'I thought, if I could get over it a bit, it would be better'. This mother chose not to tell her children at once and the evasions strained her relationship with them. Children miss their father desperately, especially at first. They need to talk about it and cry, preferably with their mother, not alone in some secret place.

Pamela's concern was that her son was alone for his father's funeral. 'He had to stand at the station and receive the coffin coming in off the train. He did have his grandparents with him, but they were, of course, totally overcome with what had happened. To me, at one of the most important times I needed to be with him, it was terrible not to be there, but I was still in hospital unaware even of what was happening.'

Andra's son would change the subject every time his father's name was mentioned. Twelve months later, when they visited the cemetery, he cried for the first time. Her daughter had always become upset when the father's name was mentioned. Another woman's son became violent with her. 'But that has passed, and now he is fine.' The problem is, of course, that the mother is in no fit condition to deal with any of this at first. She may be tempted to rush for professional help when all that is needed is the group therapy of grieving together.

Ethel Kennedy has been faced with the onerous task of raising alone eleven children, one of which was born posthumously. There was only so much time to stretch between them all. That may well account for the eldest of them being left to fend for themselves when they were perhaps in the greatest need. They must have missed their father more than the rest because they knew him better. It is no wonder that, for some time, they were unruly and gave their mother a lot of trouble.

The smaller they are, the easier the explanation. Catherine, whose husband had died in the Falklands, told her young son; 'Daddy had to go away, he wanted to come back, but he couldn't.' Susan says when her three-year-old came home from school crying: 'They say I've got no Daddy,' 'I told her, you're lucky, you've got a Mummy/Daddy.' In some ways it had been fortunate that her husband's long working hours had meant it was some time before her child asked 'When is my Daddy coming home?' Susan dealt with why he was not, gently but briefly, because: 'Sarah gets panicky if I cry.'

Wars leave a surfeit of young widows in their wake. Children become hardened to that reality as it blazes across the headlines. They are on guard: 'When my husband was reported missing on a bombing raid south of Berlin, my son said: "I don't think my Daddy's ever coming home."'

A mother alone suffers a constant fear: 'If something happened to me, what would happen to them?' Barbara said: 'At first, I wouldn't drive if I was going out to dinner. I was terrified something might happen to me.' Some mothers safeguard their children by sending them to boarding school.

'It was a hard decision, but I reasoned he would have a steady male influence and learn to stand on his own feet.'

Pamela chose to keep her son in an American school system. 'There were so many servicemen in England, they had schools set up. I felt that he had had enough disruption in his life, losing a father and moving to England. He didn't need to adjust to a new method of education as well.'

Marguerite tried to smooth over the loss of a male influence by asking her parents to join them on holiday, 'so they wouldn't feel Daddy's death set them apart'. But she would not allow any changes in their Sunday school routine. 'They never liked going, and I did not want them to view their father's death as a way out of the lessons.'

The missing presence of a father in children's lives is a continuing problem. 'I see them at parties and school events looking longingly at children with their fathers and feel so sad for them.' Catherine is trying hard to keep Daddy alive for the baby who never knew him. Constant conversational references have worked well enough for him to make the same 'My Daddy says' claims as his friends at play. They also get Daddy's car out of the garage every so often to wash and polish it. A lady who has followed a similar path says: 'Four years have passed, and my husband's influence on the family is as strong as ever.' This has been done with constant references and discussion on his views.

Bette has raised her children on Graham's philosophy and: 'There are many times I passed his photograph and asked, "How am I doing?" and I can feel him say, "Hmmm – not bad!". But sometimes I say, "I need your strength today."'

How does one counter outside influences and heartless attitudes? Susan says of her older child: 'When she started a new school, I discovered she was rated a "problem child". I asked why, and they said it was because she was fatherless. I removed her from that school and determined to find a way to pay for the private education we had originally planned.'

That empty space father has left behind looms large in all

sorts of situations. Pamela says: 'I tried taking my son out to dinner. We went in to the restaurant and ordered. Then I looked around: it was all happy families, Mums and Dads and children having a meal out together. Our own situation was brought too sharply into focus. I grabbed my son by the hand and we ran out'.

The reminders of being an incomplete family unit are constant. Some feel a new environment will provide solutions. 'Your life has to be different when you are widowed. So you have to start again, new scenes, new people'. This is not guaranteed to work either, as Louise discovered. She moved from a small flat in town to the suburbs and enrolled the boy in a local school. She did not recognize that there were three barriers against her making new friends – at least, married ones: she was young, attractive and worst of all, a widow! That hemmed her in with danger signs as far as the other mothers were concerned. She reasoned that perhaps a country life would be better and moved again. Her son was not happy there. They returned to town and settled down comfortably.

Kim Casali moved from suburbia to Monte Carlo. That did not turn out to be a suitable place to raise three British schoolchildren. She returned to their house in England but finds life there lonely. People assume that, being a celebrity, she leads a busy social life. This does not happen to be true. 'Men I meet in business are married.' Those who are not tend to shy away from her as a woman of strength.

Home cannot be the same any more. Neighbouring wives may be hostile to the widowed mum, husbands may not. There are those who arrive on the doorstep wanting to confide: 'My wife doesn't understand me'. Rose worked out a satisfactory dampener for that kind of hopeful flame. 'I don't want to either' was her reply.

She was not so quick on the uptake with an offer to sweep her chimney. In the days when the main source of heat in the home came from the fireplace, cleaning the chimney was an extra expense, not welcome on a limited income. When a neighbour offered to do it for nothing, she was delighted. He arrived to find the children up and suggested they be put to bed – 'to get them out of the way'. She then realized that there was more to this offer than the removal of a pile of soot, and put him out. From then on she called in a professional chimney sweep.

That did not mean her problems with other women's men were over. Her best friend's husband 'kept pestering me. He tried through the children, bringing them fruit.' In those days, for people short on funds, fruit was a luxury. 'I told him I didn't want to come between man and wife.' This did not put him off. Eventually Rose had to ask her father-in-law to 'see him off'.

However, not every widow wants to be that independent. Sex, or the lack of it, can cause problems. 'A woman misses a regular sex life just as much as a man.' Up to the advent of the pill, the continuation of a sex life for a widow was just as overshadowed by fear of pregnancy as that of any unmarried woman who took her chances, and possibly, less easy to explain.

'I can still remember the exact moment I began to wonder about it. I was vacuuming the bedroom, so it might have been the proximity of our bed that set me off. What was I going to do? After all, you couldn't exactly walk up to a man and say, "I'm hungry." Anyway, not twenty-five years ago.' Times do change, however. A more recent widow who went to her doctor with a series of ailments had it spelled out for her. 'What you need is SEX, he said.'

This may explain why, in earlier times, the young widow became the village prostitute. It beat taking in washing, which was then her only alternative income! This assumption of that role seems to continue in some places. One young widow reported that 'men knocked on my door any time of the night', and she was forced to move to the anonymity of a larger town to protect herself.

Women who have gone into marriage as virgins had the additional problems of no other experience to draw on. For all her needs, one felt: 'I couldn't take another man into my husband's bed'; or 'If I were promiscuous, I'd be letting him down'. However, they have a problem that will not go away easily. 'I woke up one night and found I was masturbating'; 'I knew what sex was all about now, and missed it badly'. This lady went on a sexual binge which included visits to motels, back seats of parked cars – 'I was catching up on everything I had missed before I got married.' She left her married friends' heads spinning: 'They still saw me as a wife. I seemed to be acting unfaithful – but to whom? My husband's memory? – he'd probably have applauded.'

She was dealing with a less liberal society. The appearance of respectability was paramount. 'I couldn't be seen to be sleeping around. It wasn't fair on the children. In the end, we moved out of the old neighbourhood, and also I calmed down.' One should see this sexual frenzy as similar to the wild shopping sprees in which other widows are known to indulge.

Some solve their problems at home: 'I took men to bed, but made sure they left before the childen woke up.' This had some rather indignant lovers making their exit via a window at 3.30 a.m. This strategy was understood by another mother, who said: 'I never let a man stay all night. I wouldn't want the children to find a stranger in my bed.' Torn between the natural need for a man and enjoying a sexual relationship without marriage can lead to all sorts of intrigue.

It isn't only sex one misses from a husband, it's his very male presence. This can cause trouble, if they want it – embarrassment if not. 'Some friends came visiting. I was so glad to see them. It was heaven to be enveloped by a man, to smell the male aroma of soap and aftershave. He ruined it by running his hands over my breast as he let me go. It made me wary of hugging any "friend" in future.' To have made a fuss would have ruined this friendship. 'His wife would have probably felt I rubbed against him deliberately, or there could have been a row. I couldn't cope with the upset.' What they all discover is, in any relationship that involves a widow and a man – husband or not – she will always be blamed, seen as the predator.

Physical frustration is a subject dealt with delicately in pamphlets designed for widows of any age, but particularly for young ones: 'Are keep-fit classes any good?' was a constant question put forward. With it came a reassuring reply from someone who said: 'I have been going to a music and movement class for a long time and found it absolutely marvellous. Tired as I may be, when I go, I come away feeling another person.'

There is a need to bridge this reserve and perhaps talk about the real reason why there is this excess energy to be burned. It may be fear of pity that keeps these women away from the group sessions. Why should it, when as young wives their conversations were probably enlivened with sexual discoveries and variations? Now the need is even greater. Mum is struggling to fill father's role with the children while aching for his attention on herself. She may claim that: 'This exercise has lifted me out of the mental and physical frustration'; but will that frustration ever go away? Wouldn't it be better if she could at least talk it through with women in a similar situation?

Granted, joining in the children's activities by becoming a helper helps her in other ways. She is not left alone in the empty house. She is kept out of mischief; that may be preferable to liaisons which would lead to trouble, and it is a route many prefer not to take; but: 'I get very sad, as I feel that I shall be alone for the rest of my life,' a situation very hard for a woman in her mid-thirties to accept.

Who can say which is the best way out for these young women now burdened with a double responsibility? One can understand their fearing to navigate the dangers of a second marriage with children of the first; 'I am so afraid of what will happen if I fall for someone my children do not like', said more than one. Pamela met a very eligible widower with three children. 'I'd always wanted more children, so I thought this was the solution; but my son, who knew the family and didn't much like them, said: "Forget it, mother," and I did. It wasn't that important to me; he was.'

It is interesting to note that if a widow does marry again and that marriage ends, she will revert to the family of the first marriage where they are linked by children.

Certain religions suggest a delay on a new marriage to protect the unborn child. The Jewish widow cannot marry again for ninety days. The period of waiting for a Muslim, called Iddat, is an extra half month on that. Mayayana Buddhists have to wait six months to make doubly sure there is no doubt as to who would be the new baby's natural father. One can see the sense of all of this, but not that of a learned man of the seventeenth century who cautioned that children of a second marriage might resemble the husband of the first!

Women who prefer not to take any chances on remarriage will see their children grow up and go on with their lives with mixed emotions. While there is a great sigh of relief – 'I felt like a great weight had been lifted from my shoulders when he turned twenty-one,' was echoed many times, and 'We seem to be all right now, don't we, Mummy?' said Barbara's teenage daughter – at the same time another role has been taken from the widow.

Her position in society has now to be redefined again.

8

Finance

'Suddenly I had to handle all the bills'

Many wives have never handled more than their housekeeping money before. For all but the very few who have a business manager, being left in sole financial command of however much or little they now have is a frightening responsibility. On them now depends their own and their children's security. 'I have this element of feeling terribly cheated, my life is changed, the paperwork is difficult – am I doing it right?'

All the advice that flowed around a widow unheeded when she was still in a state of shock would now be useful. But it has usually come to a halt. People feel that they have done their bit or enough time has elapsed for a widow to be getting on with her own life. Not only that, but the very people who are seen as natural father-figures advisers seem to be the ones to lead the band when it comes to mental harassment. One wonders if they are clinging to their imagined superiority.

Fortunately, their numbers are being replaced by a more open-minded generation as one lucky lady discovered. 'I went to the bank for advice; the manager was new, a young man who suggested I buy myself a luxury first.' Her modest financial fling went no further than a colour television, the very thing she and her husband had been putting off buying.

It does not follow that if a newly widowed woman is financially helpless she will stay that way. At first, struggling through paperwork which still bears her husband's handwriting, she needs sympathy, not the impatience that is usually her lot. Allowances do not seem to be made for the fact this is a woman very lately entered upon what may have been exclusively his domain. Many women, especially those in the older age bracket, have been discouraged from knowing too much. 'He'd have been happy if I never ever signed a cheque,' says Sarah, who proceeded to learn not only how to write them but to read her bank statement correctly.

Bank managers should have a little more understanding of the flush of tears that begin when these women are confronted with a bank statement. One widow reported: 'I was treated like a congenital idiot because I could not quickly grasp the complexities of my financial position.' And from another: 'Getting a cheque book in my own name was like getting blood from a stone.'

Celia had taken a business course during her husband's lifetime: 'It was important to know a little more than I did.' Considering the size of their fortune, this was extremely sensible. From the start, she made it clear she was in control. On her first visit to the bank: 'Ten men were crowded into the office. "Gentlemen," I told them, "I know you take a fee by the hour. I want you to know I know."' They were thereby warned not to take advantage.

Banking is not the only example of this harassment that leads to financial hardship. Authority, in the days of housing allocation, could make life difficult. 'Unless you were out on the street, the Council would not help.' This particular war widow had to use her tiny capital to buy a house outright. To maintain it, she brought in a housekeeper to care for her children and returned to her pre-war profession of teaching to support them.

'When you are a widow, you're taken advantage of. My brother conned me into loaning him £5,000. I never got it back.' How sad for a close member of the family to show so little pity.

Frances Anne's first effort to be independent of her parents, who kept an eye on her, became another example of how the 'little widow' can be preyed upon. An unscrupulous estate agent pocketed the deposit on the first house she had chosen and departed. Her next attempt did not seem to begin any more auspiciously since she was refused a mortgage.

By that time single women were able to obtain home loans, so this did not make sense, especially since she had proof of a pension enough for herself and her son. In answer to her question, the building society's clerk had the temerity to tell her, as a young widow: 'A slice has been cut off your loaf.' She was a bad risk! It was a none-too-subtle suggestion that she might get careless enough to have another baby, which would drain her pension and, therefore, her ability to repay the mortgage. Fortunately she found another building society with a more humane approach.

The innocence enjoyed through the protection of a husband gets dashed away in widowhood. Pamela had a particularly nasty experience: 'While I was still unconscious in the hospital a lawyer was appointed for me. I had no reason to doubt the man as he came highly recommended. Preparations began for a court case against the company for whom the truck-driver had worked. It was when the lawyer suggested all sorts of things like greasing my scars to make me look worse and that I limp on to the stand to give evidence, I began to be concerned. By then I was recovering and beginning to look normal again, so it all seemed dishonest. I had a lot to learn.

'Then I was told the other side were willing to settle out of court. When the lawyer named a figure he avoided looking me straight in the eye as I asked if it seemed fair. However, according to the US practice he would get one third of the settlement, so I had every reason to suppose he would do his best. I could not judge the amount of money he proposed I accept, nor could I turn to anyone for advice. No one I knew had ever been involved in such a situation. What price do you put on the loss of a husband and the injuries I had suffered? I dreaded going to court, I was never very good at lying. I settled for what I later discovered was a joke figure.

'It appeared that the lawyer had taken his cut not only from me, but from the opposing side for getting me to settle so fast and for so little. Of course I should never have accepted the first offer, but how can one bargain? I felt that as I was recovering and my son had been spared, I should count my blessings. That money never meant much to me. I had a pension from the Navy and the settlement began to be frittered away. I couldn't think about "tomorrow". Mine had been snatched away from me.'

Many widows discover that for more than one reason their financial pot is not as full as they expected. Bette Hill's life-style had to change gear – downward. Their mansion was sold because: 'My old Graham thought everyone was as nice as himself.' From this, one must assume she suffered certain problems connected with money after her husband's death.

Another woman, whose husband had been stabbed by thieves when he attempted to protect the shop where he was working, was offered the most measly sum in compensation. 'The owner had run away and left my husband there; he was not only wealthy, but a friend. This made me bitter. I told him, "I don't want to see you again."'

Debbie Reynolds may have married a millionaire, but when he died she found herself with 1.2 million dollars of debts pinned to her shoulders. She danced her way out of them by appearing in theatres all over the USA. Since then, her fortunes have been even more restored by some shrewd buying at film studio auctions. She has cornered a fair proportion of the market in movie memorabilia.

After Yasmine had paid for the funeral expenses, she discovered there was only £45 left in the bank. She wired her husband's partners in Pakistan for more funds and was told nothing else was due: 'I had been left with no insurance. I had to do something quickly. I was going to get a job and survive even if I had to become a traffic warden.'

Her only assets, the house and car, had to be sold at once. 'I halved the money and told my three sons, "I'm twice as old as you are, so half goes in trust for all of you to share, the rest is mine."' To provide a home for them, she bought a small flat with her part of the money.

For all her husband's careful preparations in those extra months he managed to keep alive, Joan R. ended up leaving India with nothing but a box of jewellery. She passed the deeds of her house to a business associate who was staying on. He promised to settle her affairs, but 'everything just went with him.'

One woman was confronted with a will that left everything to the son of her husband's first marriage. 'Everything' included her home, for which she had contributed a half-share. She had no papers to prove it. This marriage had been doomed almost as it began. She had rebounded from a shock divorce after thirty-three years. The trauma of that divorce case made her hesitant to enter another battle in the courts to secure what was rightfully hers. She was, therefore, legally out on the street. It took several jobs, including teaching at night school, to restore her security.

However dazzled by love a woman is, it is as well for her to remember that certain legal formalities regarding property should be put on paper so that if she is widowed, she is protected and can survive financially. It can resolve those unknown debts. If they assume alarming proportions, but she owns the house, hopefully there will be enough from the sale of it to put a smaller roof over her head.

Owned or rented, the house can produce income; a large one can become a guest house; even the spare room will hold a lodger. This is what Rose would eventually do.

'I made up my mind we would manage somehow.' In the 1940s, before the advent of Social Security, Rose had a big problem. She had received very little help from what was then called the Public Assistance Office. They said her case would have to be put to a committee. In those days, the world was made up of committees of do-gooders. All too often, they were more full of their own self-importance than compassion. Smugly complacent, they seemed heartless and lacking in understanding of what it was like to be without. It is questionable how much they really helped, or whether they did their bit to continue to foster a generation of bitter people divided into 'them and us'.

This particular committee reckoned without Rose: 'They sat there in their fur coats and lounge suits (signs of affluence in the 1940s) asking me questions like, "What did I have?"' She told them; only enough to bury her husband. Whereupon one woman suggested they allow Rose 2*s.* 11*d.* a week (approximately 15*p.*) until her pension came in. She would then have to repay it. She would also qualify for second-hand clothes for her children through the Women's Voluntary Services, but they would have to be handed back as soon as they were outgrown. They saw no humour in Rose's grim reply that the clothes would not be handed back because the children would wear them out before they outgrew them.

When it came, her pension was 18*s.* (approximately 85*p.*) per week of which 10*s.* (50*p.*) was for her, 5*s.* (25*p.*) was for the first child and 3*s.* (15*p.*) for the second. With it was a reminder that she must try to help herself. The question was – how? 'My doctor had already said to me, "Please don't leave your children and go out to work. They've lost their father, don't let them think they've lost their mother."

The solution was to rent out the spare room, complete with a morning and evening meal. She was required to notify the Pension Office of the change in her finances. 'They came to inspect my circumstances and prepared to deduct the lodgers' rent from my pension.' When she protested against the unfairness of it, since there was wear and tear on her home and furnishings to consider, they did not agree.

Rose changed tactics. If she took in lodgers on a bed-and-breakfast basis, it earned less money but less would be deducted from her pension book. She notified the authorities. 'My book was always being changed.' The unfairness of the system at that time included the fact that working married women enjoyed a more favourable tax deduction and had advantages over widows.

As soon as her children were of school age, Rose gave up her lodgers and found a part-time job at their school. 'A guinea (£1.05) a week and free dinner'. Of course, her pension book was changed again.

Her son pitched in to help as soon as he could. He had a paper round and a weekend job at a bakery on a factory estate nearby. 'He would bring home his wages, pour the money on the table and say "There you are, Mum."'

As soon as a vacancy at that school occurred, she applied for a full-time job. 'It was longer hours but more money.' By the time she quit, sixteen years later, her salary was £3.14*s*. (£3.70). She was still not able to afford her daughter the career she wanted. 'She would have liked to train as a hairdresser.' Parents then not only had to pay for the apprenticeship, but help with spending money as well. Rose had to convince the girl that the idea was not practicable. 'She would have wanted pretty clothes and I wouldn't be able to help.'

Rose has come through her trials and tribulations with a great sense of achievement: 'I was proud to have been able to keep out of debt.' And nowadays she has the pleasure of lavishing on her grandchildren some of the luxuries she had to deny their parents.

The war widows of the Second World War were also suffering a drop in their standard of living. In addition, red tape tangles caused complications when their hubands were reported missing, not killed. To the agonizing suspense was added the worry of how they would get by financially.

'I took in sewing'; 'I took in lodgers'; 'I went out to work'; this all too often meant leaving a small child in the care of someone else.

Marjorie was expecting a baby when the news came that her RAF husband was missing on a thousand-bomber raid: 'I can remember being very frightened as to how I was going to exist.' The news was followed by a letter, hardly understandable in her state; nor probably to anyone else but the War Office:

> The regulations do not provide for payment of a temporary allowance to be continued at family allowance rate for more than a period of seventeen weeks and that any subsequent payments must be based on the rate of pension which would be payable had your husband been reported as a fatal casualty.

Did this mean she had money to live on?

In her case, a shower of letters went back and forth because, although he was promoted to the rank of sergeant, 'his pay was not increased sufficiently to grant any higher allotment'. Looking back, Marjorie realizes: 'I must have been on my knees writing and pleading not to have my pension reduced.' There were no facilities to send Social Service visitors either to counsel, minister sympathy, or suggest how women like this might carry on. Such a luxury was yet to come. To be fair, it could not be expected in wartime conditions. When the suffering is at its worst, help is least available.

Marjorie was one of the lucky ones who managed to squeeze a tiny degree of compassion from the Air Ministry. In August 1942, she received a letter to say: 'As you are expecting a child an extra 8*s*.6*d*. (42½*p*.) has been authorized.'

History has a way of repeating itself when it comes to wars, even if the amounts of money marginally increase. Ellen's husband had been making a good living when he was called back in for the Korean War in 1950. He left with a dreadful prophecy: 'Wars have wrecked so many homes. I hope it never does this to us.'

'Things began to get hard for me from the time he went away. I kept thinking this war will soon be over and my husband will be home again.' Instead, Ellen was in training for what was to come: Rifleman James Porter's name is to be found inscribed on the United Nations Memorial in Pusan, Korea.

Ellen was in dire financial straits: she received no rent allowance and had to draw on her own savings. It became a struggle to survive. 'I was very bitter at what the army had done to my family. Knowing I could never buy my children the bare necessities of life, it was indeed a trying time.' Because Ellen was pregnant when her husband left, she had the additional responsibility of the baby. Until the prisoner of war exchange in 1953, there was still the faint hope that he was not lost, and so whatever compensation she was due as a widow was delayed. By November 1954 the War Office had decided on presumption of death for missing soldiers and Ellen was officially a war widow. She received an additional 49*s*.6*d*. (£2.45) for her three children and then, some weeks later, a rent allowance: 'This made things much easier for me.'

Hilda had to learn about her husband's business if she was to survive, since this was her livelihood and 'he wanted me to run it'. One of her sons is an accountant, but she wanted to be independent and went straight to various official departments. 'I will get brainy about it all before long. I will know by the end of this year just how things are and I will be a whole lot wiser too. For a couple of months, I did not keep any records.' This was part of the usual 'Does it matter?' syndrome which affects so many widows.

Susan is of a generation where help always seems on hand. She expected someone from the authorities to come forward, but not even a social worker appeard. 'Finance was very difficult for me at first.' This could be one of those examples of a victim slipping through yet another hole in that 'net'. Her financial problems were compounded by the fact that she could only have a preliminary death certificate until the court established the 'cause of death'. This meant no pension and no insurance settlement, and it was a whole year before that case came to court.

Luckily Susan had some funds of her own, and help came from her mother. Then a neighbour told her about a job going at his place of business. 'I was thankful I didn't have to go through an interview and explain everything.' Her mother-in-law, who lived nearby, helped with the children and in this manner she was able to keep going. Eventually someone, not from the authorities, told her to take her husband's insurance stamps to the appropriate office. This started help rolling in her direction. One must ask, though, had she been completely without funds, family or a friend to offer a job, how would she have managed to support those two young children in the interim?

When it was proved that Susan's husband's death was not his fault, the insurance money began to come in, and this allowed her to give up her job and return home to the children, who were in need of their mother. 'I hope to have a business of my own one day.' One hopes she succeeds.

Mary, who is now a town councillor, with her talent for helping people, rounds off this chapter with some excellent and basic advice: 'Be aware of financial commitments. I found an unused diary and converted it into an income-and-expenditure statement. Each year is divided into its twelve months and each month's liabilities clearly defined, e.g. gas bill, water rate, phone bill, house insurance, car tax, TV licence, etc. Total income for the year is tabled at the beginning. I found it useful to use a calculator (I had to learn this 'skill') as it made the arithmetic much easier.'

Which proves that Do It Yourself is not limited to putting up shelves! Staying in control of your money, however much or little there is, is better than floundering in a sea of financial woe.

9

Coping

'Learn who you are'

Widows have to come to terms with this new chapter of their lives. There is a great gaping void to fill. Some have obligations left they must first fulfil which gives them a little time to adjust.

The Battle of Britain widow feels that her upbringing stood her in good stead: 'I had always been taught to accept the good and bad in life.'

No one should allow their life to come to a screeching halt. One eminently sensible woman adopted the philosophy: 'I probably had as much of my life left to live.' Her will may have wavered for a while when it looked as though death had come to stay. She lost her husband, mother, brother and sister in quick succession. That made her even more determined to make her life one long holiday. 'John would never have wanted me to be miserable.' At home, she is a whirlwind of activity, has already decorated her whole house and a winter project was a pond for her garden. Both jobs were completed with the aid of instruction books. 'Anyone can do anything if they set their mind to it.'

Wise advice, which leaves no room for excuses of any kind. A lack of education can be remedied. One lady studied for and passed the exam for her High School Diploma, something she had deserted in her youth for marriage. From there, it is an easy step into college and one degree can lead to another. Jehan Sadat read for a doctorate in Arabic poetry at Cairo University. It is all too easy to say: 'When you come home with your degree – who will be happy for you?' The answer can only be – 'yourself'. Personal satisfaction is a wonderful thing.

You are a person in your own right. You need to 'learn who you are' not because you are without a husband, but because you are You. Therefore, as one widow says: 'My minister said it was time I had some goals in my life, and it made sense'. And while it may seem drastic to some, another widow had this to say: 'I took off my wedding ring. I didn't like the big "W" hanging over my head.' She was at least preparing to assume her new identity. No one claims it is easy. The object is to try.

You may have been happy with your personality as 'a wife' who fitted in with her husband. But it may not be the one that fits a widow as comfortably. Having discovered that friends fade and established social contacts belonged solely to his presence, you may feel the need for things to change.

The doctor's widow had added pressures. Ministry of Health regulations meant that the locum taking her husband's place had to be replaced by someone permanent after three months: 'I remember sitting in his surgery (he actually died there) and interviewing all those people – seventy applied.' She was still not through with her duties. The village wanted to open a fund to build a memorial in his name: 'You must remember the patients are mourning him as well,' said the nurse who had been on duty there. How could she refuse them? So great and immediate was the response that within a year she attended the opening.

Beattie and her husband Jack de Leon had been synonymous with the famous 'Q' theatre at Kew Green. 'I must go on. I've got to go on,' she vowed when her husband died. This was not easy since they were negotiating for the sale of the theatre at the time of his death. She had to continue with the arrangements even thought it could have meant the end of her drama classes. This was most unfortunate since some of the best-known names in acting had passed across her stage. With such a reputation, it was inevitable that someone would come forward. In Beattie's case, it was Richmond Adult Education Authority who provided her with the premises to continue.

Thoughts of her husband were what finally pulled Evelyn le Chêne back into a useful life: 'I had to get a job, I thought Pierre would be cross with me if I did not.' Her first one was a high-powered executive role, but she was not happy when her true interest was on the subject of defence. She switched to writing about it: 'Pierre would have asked me, "What kept you so long?"'

Circumstances can hurry the process along. Doctor El Said was friendless after her husband's assassination and also short of money. 'Everything in Iraq had been confiscated.' But she was fortunate in having a good education which included five languages. She went to work for the Arabic Section of the BBC.

Examining what one can do best is often the lead back to a more 'normal' life. Barbara was lucky to have Sheila Hancock as a friend. She had gone through widowhood and saw that Barbara needed a push back into the world. She was about to direct a play. It was the one written by Terence Rattigan in which a wife dying of leukemia was keeping it from her husband who was keeping it from her. She offered that part to Barbara who admits: 'It did require immense concentration.'

That of course is the best possible medicine any widow can take. A role in a play or film has nothing to do with what has happened in real life. Maureen O'Sullivan, who played Jane in *Tarzan* early in her career, relates how: 'I was doing *Never Too Late* when John died. My work saved me. I knew that somehow I had to go out and perform, and if I missed a single performance, it would have been harder. I had to push to go on. Acting, for me, offered the Great Escape.

'When someone dies, you don't know how to behave. People don't know what to say or how to treat you in a moment of crisis, and you don't know just how to react. I didn't know exactly how I was supposed to be. But every night for those few hours on stage, I didn't have to cope. I didn't have to think about how I was supposed to be. I knew. I had words that were familiar, moves that were familiar. The others never stepped out of their characters. In the midst of all my personal trauma, my part in the play was a secure world. By the time the tour was finished, I'd had enough time to get hold, and my work saved my life.'

Acting isn't the only outlet. Sally Oppenheimer, MP, lost herself in the complications of politics at Westminster as quickly as she could. Pat Seed forced herself to carry on her fund raising project for cancer victims similar to herself, when her husband was killed at the Abbeystead Pumping Station explosion.

Sarah's husband's position had given her a world full of receptions, Royal garden parties and the like. This came to a stop, but her circle of acquaintances has enlarged because 'No one is ever a stranger. I like to chat, even in a bus queue. I'm amazed how lonely people are; staggered by what they say and how all they really want to do is talk to someone.'

Every day she finds something to do, if it is only limited to meeting someone at the local department store for tea or coffee. There is also an old family friend nearby. Their children went to school together. 'He is a widower, so we sit and talk about our partners.' There is also a kind neighbour and friends who phone her all the time. She has learned to be a good-value guest with a smiling face. 'No one is interested in you if you are miserable.' What her generation calls 'little weeps' are done in private.

Her only complaint is about people who say what she considers silly things like: '"I couldn't live alone" – what do they suggest I do?'

It may be that all these years there has been another personality longing to get out of its wifely trappings. One Old Dear had acceded to all her husband's Victorian principles. She was expected not to leave home without his permission except to go shopping. An occasional treat was tea at a married daughter's home. Widowed in her seventies, her sense of independence broke through. First she began to smoke (something he had frowned on). Then, she went out into the world via an old people's club, thoroughly enjoying all the activities that they offered such as theatre visits and trips to the coast. She was not grounded till her nineties.

Marjory has improved her lonely lot by making friends in a like situation. They have monthly meetings and discuss different problems which relate to themselves. However, she still finds living alone a bind: 'You begin to lose your sense of humour. No one to giggle at over TV for instance.'

There are a whole new set of rules to learn, all of which may not be appealing but have to be accepted: 'You have to learn to grow a thicker skin . . .'

Katie Boyle discovered: 'Work was my way out. Four days after the funeral I decided to honour a contract that would take me away for nine weeks, doing a show in a different town every night. I don't remember a thing about that period of my life, where I went, what I did. It turned into a complete blank.' What she does remember are the many who said: 'You're lucky to have been so busy.' Those with a job have a continuity to their life which does not relate to their husband's death and they do better. 'I felt it was important to work' was echoed many times.

Mary Hemingway eventually found her salvation in: 'Work, lovely satisfying work.' Directed by her husband's will to administer his estate, all she could manage at first was the top layer of manuscripts he left behind. Eventually, she was able to get his last book published posthumously.

Diana Raymond had worked alongside, but not with, her husband which helped her work through the first part of her widowhood. After four starts, she chose to make the subject of her next novel a widow, and was able to pour a lot of her own emotions into the dialogue. It was like a reassurance to herself when she had a friend tell the heroine: 'Believe me, the anguish does pass.' Since then, she has tackled less morbid themes.

Mary Martin was held up on her return to her career because grief had taken its toll of her voice. Then, just as she was beginning to find her way forward and was lined up as hostess of a chat show, she was involved in a car accident. There was doubt she would ever walk again. 'Was my career over – again?' Her first goal was to rise from that hospital bed to visit Janet Gaynor, her best friend who had been even more badly smashed up in the same crash. The success of this determination to think positively eventually carried her back into her career.

Norma coped by keeping frantically busy: 'Even if you sweep streets, you must keep busy.' She is unstoppable, moving house, renovating, running for a job which was at first 'like a gift from heaven'. A blood transfusion service was being started. As a wartime VAD, she knew just how to do it. Everything would have been fine if it had not been part-time. This meant there were still spaces in her day to be filled in. It became a short-term solution. A friend suggested she join her in a business venture. It prospered and was sold as a going concern. She was persuaded into another one which ended up with the same successful result, except that it left Norma with a longing for something else to do. Just at that time, circumstances arose which gave her opportunities to keep on the move. A sister had gone to live in USA and offered constant invitations. Her sons went to work abroad and grandchildren arrived who needed a visiting Grandma. Still, Norma insists: 'Life is not a fairy story.' What she cannot come to terms with is her unhappy ending.

Marie was equally restless. Her family took turns visiting her in America. She came to Britain several times. She wrestled with decisions. 'I knew I needed to sell the house but didn't want to, we had done so much work on it together.'

Pamela came back to London. 'I needed a place to live, I couldn't stay with family too long. Once you have had your own home, it is impossible to share.' Her greatest problem for a while was finding a flat with a kitchen large enough to take her enormous American freezer.

Bette Hill had made a difficult decision early on to get on

with her life and not be buffered by the many friends who surrounded her from the moment the news was out: 'A week after the accident, I had to say to myself, the children must go back to school. We've got to start again. Monday is the beginning of the week – we start on Monday. Everybody who would not normally be here must leave.' It was a brave act but, as she says: 'Graham taught me to be strong. He had so much guts, dedication and love for his fellow man and was an example to us all.'

Eventually, she moved to a smaller house and felt the need to do something different: 'I took a job at the same health club where I was a member. I worked at the reception desk, but after a while, as people came out and kept slapping those soggy wet towels across the counter as they left, I began to ask myself: What am I doing here? I'm Mrs Graham Hill, people used to queue up to meet me with Graham. We were so humble, for all this attention given us.' Bette gave up the job and went back to being a member only. She has had the satisfaction of seeing her children grow up and go on to their own careers. One daughter has gone to live abroad. Bette has kept her connections with car racing, not only because her son is now driving, but she has stayed a member of The Doghouse, a fund-raising charity run by the women of that world.

Cynthia remained in her mother's home for quite some time. She did not really expiate her guilt until she met a Yogi: 'I thought he could teach me something. He felt I was receptive to ideas. I had twelve sessions with him. He took no money from me but put me back together more or less by kicking me in the pants. He said, "Pull yourself together – your duty as a human being is to perform at your best."' This is good advice for all readers of this book. She moved to Washington, took a flat, got herself involved in tennis clubs and the usual social whirl and went on to work at the Smithsonian Institute.

One lady freely admitted: 'I was a terrible load on my children at the beginning.' She went to stay with her daughter.

'Then, one day, my sister came to say she would go home with me. After a few days, she came in with a cup of tea in the morning and said, "I'm going today." She made me pull myself together.' Again, the short sharp shock! Very necessary, however brutal it seems at the time. This woman had a bonus in having a son prepared to help. If she would give up the large house and move into something more convenient to town, he would live at home while he was at University. 'This was my recovery – I was needed.'

Usually, it is when the sons go away to University that the widow feels deserted and problems arise. 'My son said to me, "Now you'd better learn to drive and stand on your own two feet." Every time I had a lesson I cried at the reasons why I was having to learn to drive. The instructor finally shouted at me, "You're going to drive," and I did.'

Betty was jolted back into the world by her stay in a mental home. When she was well enough, she returned to her mews house. She now is very busy, is writing a novel but still finds it hard when she entertains. 'I resent seeing any other man sitting in "his" chair.'

A widow with young children has to pull herself together fast for their sake. One left with four youngsters had to make a choice between the care of her large house and the garden. Her solution proved propitious. The woman she hired to do the housework was a widow of some standing who offered practical advice. 'Get through the first six months and you will be all right.' This worked out fine and she began to be able to view the future in less sombre tones. 'A friend was taking a hostess cookery course. She asked me to join her. It was good to be with people who knew nothing about me and I enjoyed it.' The process of accepting had begun.

With children still at home, the only hours to fill are while they are at school. Anne, the only suicide's widow interviewed who was not racked with guilt, said: 'He was a manic-depressive. He chose to get away from his family to set them free. I sensed as I reported him missing that he was dead.' She became involved in several voluntary projects. The most important was to serve on the Board of Directors of the Los Angeles Suicide Prevention Center. She hoped her efforts could prevent other wives suffering the same fate as herself. For this work and being on commissions as varied as the Conservation of Energy and the Metropolitan Opera, in 1975 she was awarded the Los Angeles County Human Relations Commission commendation for her services.

Those widows who find time hanging too heavily on their hands might do well to follow the piece of advice most freely handed to bored widows: 'Join something.' Certainly, the key to coping is keeping busy: 'It soaks up time.' Bridge players seem to have the easiest outs. Pairs made up for a game do not have to be husbands and wives: 'A bridge game is one of my favourite ways to push a button and escape' – Mrs L. B. Johnson. This does not occupy all her time since she could never be regarded as a lady of leisure. There are multiple business interests to oversee which include radio and television stations. Her most precious project is the conservation of wild flowers in the American countryside. To that end she has donated sixty acres of land along the Colorado River in East Texas.

Escape buttons do not necessarily have labels on them, nor do they stand in a row. It is up to the widow to 'get off her backside' and find them.

10

Merry widowhood versus remarriage

'I'm kinda dating and it's strange'

According to one psychologist, there are two categories of widows: those who are determined to remarry and those who cannot bear the idea. Those who want a second husband seem to want someone as much as possible like the man they remember. Those who never expect to find someone as good or are frightened they'll end up with one as bad prefer not to try at all.

There are the doubters: 'I thought I'd never have that feeling of being able to totally commit and to give and receive . . . the feeling of being in love' – Elizabeth Taylor, remembering how she felt after the death of Michael Todd. Like other women she was to discover differently. As one said of her second marriage: 'My life was now like a glass of vintage champagne compared to a mug of tepid milk and water.'

It has been claimed that a widow stands a better chance of developing a serious relationship than an unmarried woman. A widow is used to having a man around. She has more to miss: 'I went on holiday with a single friend. I was very aware of the tables of couples. She didn't even notice them.' It is especially hard on the women who enjoyed fluttering around and catering to their men. And on those whose husbands had been their buffer against the outside world. It is a giant step coming back into it without his protection: 'If you have been a busy wife and mum, you've lost that kind of confidence. I was hesitant coming out on to that different scene.'

Where do they go if they want to find a replacement? In biblical times, it was the duty of the surviving brother to provide for his dead brother's family. One can see where there would be some pressure on his part to see her safely into another man's arms and removed from his responsibility!

But today, how does a widow set about it? The Saturday night dances of her youth are out. So are the 'goings on' at the Rugger Club, or any other get-together in the intermediary meeting places of the younger generation. There are also wine bars, discos, pubs and the bars of hotels. These are of little help. Men who congregate there are more likely to be looking for 'a bit on the side': only a temporary respite which can lead to further heartbreak. 'I learned the hard way that those charmers were not genuine. All they wanted to do was get me into bed.'

There are clubs which make no pretence of being other than social occasions for matchmaking. For the widow, intent on a new marriage, they may be her answer. Getting in is not so easy. Quite a few of them ration their entry to balance numbers between the unmarried and the divorced. Such clubs have disadvantages because 'the men were mostly divorced, with problems and maintenance. They wanted a ready shoulder to cry on. The widowers were snapped up fast.'

When the 'looking' gets serious, so does the competition. As one woman in her forties said: 'You don't want an older man, you want someone to be a companion. Most of the men of my age want a dolly bird on their arm who can have a child by them, so they can say, "Look how clever I am!"' Another, who did not see her sixties as reason to give up, went further: 'All the men I meet either have angina or bad hip joints.'

Could this be the reason for the resurgence of the tea dance? They can provide a more gentle and less competitive, no-strings-attached entry into this new social world. 'It's all very romantic.' After the familiarity of marriage and the years of being taken for granted, the excitement and the flattery can turn a widow's head regardless of her age. In addition, since there is no membership, one can stay incognito if necessary!

Some widows advertise in personal columns of magazines, but changes in word usage in just one generation mean that something like: 'Young gay 69, lively, good conversationalist' can bring ludicrously inappropriate replies. But box numbers can be used to protect one's privacy. One should never get desperate enough to dispense with them.

Even from the sixty-plus pinnacle, it can be necessary to state in those advertisements: 'No affairs please'. It does not follow that these women are adverse to sexual encounters; they just wish it were not so quickly assumed that this is the one need they have. As one confessed: 'Even my son-in-law made advances to me.'

'Most widows do want some male company', says a seventy-seven-year-old, who related how, at a party, she was seated next to a gentleman on his own. He was charming and treated her like a lady. They danced the whole evening and for the first time in four years she enjoyed herself: 'I felt like a person again.'

Married friends may try to help by producing what they feel are potential partners. This overture should be welcomed, even if she feels she is only there to tidy up the head count at the dinner table. It is still better than being left out. Some friends have been known to arrange blind dates. A widow quickly becomes cautious over such remarks as 'He'd be perfect for you.' She can never be sure if this is a genuine opinion or an attempt to draw her back into the married circle. What is worse is the assumption by a lot of men that she is dessert after dinner when she is taken home. As a faithful wife, a woman has to re-learn the art of 'dealing' with a strange man. Those who married young are often particularly unsure because they have never reached their potential as single women.

Solicitous and caring male friends who are there in early widowhood – quite often the husband's best friend – should not be confused with husband material, however great the temptation. While the woman may crave the continuation of a man in her life, she must remember that there is a ritual to mating which is rarely bridged quickly. 'Marry in haste, repent in leisure' does not only apply to first marriages. There is danger ahead for a widow who is too eager.

Think carefully when considering a replacement for the husband who is no longer there. Forget excuses like: 'The children need a father.' A wrong choice of man can lead to a mother being as unhappy as she was when she was first widowed. The gap between boyfriend and husband is wide. It is all too easy to scare off a boyfriend by expecting from him the commitment of a husband or the same loyalty too fast: 'It took me a long time to accept that I could not interrupt the boyfriend's business conferences.'

A father's advice to his daughter forty years ago may sound a little old-fashioned by today's standards, but it is worth repeating: 'If you are widowed when you have lost the bloom of youth and you are quite comfortably placed you can rest assured that it is what you offer that the man is after, not you, so never allow yourself to be flattered that it is you he seeks.' More's the pity that this widow did not listen: her second marriage failed and she lost her pension rights from her first husband as well.

However desperate is the need for 'someone to love – someone to belong to' one should remember that 'A good act is hard to follow'. The same rules of caution should be applied in a second marriage as the first. Second husbands are not likely to change the habits they exhibit as single men because they have married an 'experienced' widow.

'I didn't even date anybody,' says Maureen O'Hara. 'Who would want to put up with a woman who's constantly talking about Charlie Blair? He was such a wonderful man.'

'I still love him,' says Jehan Sadat, 'and I can't imagine that anything can replace him. I don't have any such ideas in my mind. All I have to do is keep myself busy all the time.'

Love takes a long time dying, and if the marriage has been

happy the woman can be more in love with her husband in those later years than in the first sexual flush of romance. A widow considering remarriage will cause a lot of comment. 'Married friends said "Do", widowed friends said "Take care"'. Widows have more to give up than a young bride. It could be pension, inheritance, business control that she hesitates to relinquish.

Large insurance policies can make a widow richer than she ever was as a wife. A woman who had young children at the time of her husband's death offers this advice: 'Don't marry again unless you are sure he is a kind man and really likes your children. Question his motives. Safer to have a little affair (take precautions please!) than make a permanent mistake.'

Therefore, once a widow establishes herself in a new life, either by moving to a more congenial location or opening up different horizons on her present scene, she could do as well to stay merry rather than remarry. 'There's a lot to be said for living on your own as if you've always been single.'

Many a young widow has suffered from mothers who seem to expect them to return to a single virginal state. This was Kathleen Kennedy's problem. Her marriage had already caused ripples of embarrassment in her family. The Duke of Devonshire's son was not a Catholic. She escaped back to England where, to distinguish her from the wife of the new heir, Kathleen was known as The Lady Hartington. As she made a merry way through the London Society of that time, she began to be known as 'The Widow Hartington'. The giddy round of parties stopped when she fell in love with a married man, a danger all widows should try to avoid. Nor was he a Catholic. She took him to France to plead her case with her father. Their plane was caught in bad weather and crashed. She was brought back to be buried beside her husband in the family plot at Chatsworth, England.

Once upon a time, it was necessary to hide an affair. In today's climate there is no such reluctance. In fact, this or a steady relationship seems preferable to many women. Even the older ones, whose upbringing may have dictated that marriage was the only route to her bed, now 'keep house' with the new man in their lives. It makes for fewer complications when their estates are divided. Nor is there any age limit to this life-style. One woman, at seventy-five, rediscovered an old school friend, a widower of eighty-one. They have chosen to live together in his council flat. 'Why should we be lonely?' Why indeed! It would appear that only their grown children disapprove.

Another woman tried to solve this loneliness by going to a marriage bureau. Her interest was companionship more than marriage: 'Because you have to make an entirely new life, particularly if your friends are married. There are lots of things they can't do because they have a husband.' This is a fascinating switch of opinion and, in many ways, a delightful two-fingered gesture at certain condescending married women from which they all suffer. It can put an end to the synthetic 'poor yous' tossed constantly in their direction.

This marriage bureau proved a great success: 'I met five men through it and had a wonderful time for eighteen months.' This may make the reader envisage a swinger. They would be wrong. This lady is solid, upright and white-haired. However, her great sense of fun was sorely in need of someone responsive to her humour. When she met such a person, he became very special. 'He made a terrific fuss of me, restored me to normal womanhood.' Sadly, the man died. She had no heart to return to the bureau and began to build a different shape to her life.

Shirley has kept her neighbour's eyes popping as she has gone through her merry widowhood. Circumstances, not promiscuity, have caused her line of lovers. However, they have all left their mark on the house she bought with her husband as a young bride. This is her base – her security – something she will never give up; it will go to her son.

The parade began with a co-worker at the office, who was more a man to fill the gap after her husband's death. This is 'danger time'. Too many widows are tempted into a new marriage because they miss a 'man about the house'. This particular one brought order to Shirley's neglected garden where little had been done since her husband's illness began. One corner had become an unrestrained mass of rambling roses. One wonders if they pricked his conscience, because he had no sooner brought them to order than he deserted her for his wife.

It must be made clear that she never set out to be a husband-stealer. The men have come to her by their own choice. It could be her very independent mind which attracts them, or do they perhaps think that they will master her? It hasn't happened yet.

The next on the scene could only share her with duty to his wife, but she got the largest part of his time until a fatal heart attack. By now her boss, who had been an admiring watcher on the sidelines, made his move: 'Determined to have me before anyone else came along.' Shirley was fond enough of the man to agree. She is much too sensible to let her emotions run away into ecstatic love: 'He built a rather splendid addition on to the house.' They shared some happy years before he died of cancer.

She met her present man on holiday. They liked each other well enough to want to continue the association; he came to stay, unafraid of the fatalities in her past which the neighbours were quick to list. He appears to have broken her run of bad luck with men. His contribution to the home so far: 'A spectacular garden display of waterfalls and fountains.' Much as she may be against marriage, Shirley prefers a steady relationship with a man because she, like many others, knows: 'The world is not built for single people.'

Through all of this, her son has stayed amused, and secure in the fact that he is 'number one'. He is by now out of boarding school and into his own home and career. Shirley agrees with some of the other mothers left with a child of similar age: 'When he reached twenty-one, it was as if a heavy load had been removed from my shoulders.'

A mother's natural protectiveness of her young can cause a mental struggle when she considers a new marriage. If her philosophy has been to follow her husband's influence, she may wish it to continue. The advent of a stepfather may bring a conflict of ideas which causes unrest. There are added difficulties to consider. A boy raised to be 'Mama's little man' will resent the change. They should also realize that nubile teenage daughters running round the house half-dressed can be seen by the new man as a sexual challenge, not 'Daddy's little girls – growing up'. The baby who has grown into its father's image is a constant reminder of a short-lived marriage that very often had grown no blemishes. This memory can cloud the reason for the quarrels which may arise in a new marriage so that they are not seen as part of the adjustment.

A widow venturing into marriage a second time around is more likely to be very independent as a wife. Having learned that death can bring impermanence to marriage, she will not usually devote herself as fully to the second husband. However much she loves him, she knows already what it is like to be alone and from the first seems to steel her emotions against this happening again.

It would be hard to formulate the ideal second husband, especially for a widow with children. Equally, what may be seen as an advantage of a new marriage by a mother, may not be the same to her children. They have to be considered. The Muslim attitude to remarriage is romantically inclined in favour of a widow. It is a blessing to follow their leader who married one. Her name, Khadija, has become an honourable choice for a daughter.

Wisely, some women prefer not even to start looking until their children have grown. Advantages have to be balanced against hazards. A son who has been sole male of the household will feel challenged: 'I found my son and my new husband were constantly competing, trying to top each other in word and deed. I put a very firm stop to that and we all settled down.'

Teenagers have problems regardless of whether they have a

natural father or a stepfather. Mother is usually the one in between. It is less easy to deal with in the latter case. When theories on child-raising have been formulated by parents as children grow, they are more workable if both have the same rights. 'I cannot be two parents, and they need two, but no "step" can substitute', says one. Rose agrees: 'I would not have been able to sit back and let someone tell my children what to do.'

It is as well to remember all the time that the man who comes into the widow's home wants the widow for his wife. The children are accepted of necessity: 'part of the package deal'. That is not to suggest dislike – but be prepared. A bachelor will not have the training needed to exercise his tolerance with rearing a child; that comes with having been there as they have grown: 'We were all too much for an introverted bachelor, who tried, but curbed high spirits. No one looks back on childhood very happily, but everyone puts on a good face in the winter of our years.' When they grew up these children went to live abroad. No one will ever know if they would have stayed closer to home in different circumstances.

A man who has reared children will have seen this as an experience that he can easily repeat, but it may not work on someone else's child, as Ruth found out. She looked for security, emotional as well as financial, in her new marriage. He was 'the first unattached man I had met. He wined and dined me at the best places. I was flattered. I felt I'd never have to work again.' This man was considerably older than Ruth, and already had grandchildren.

Her own teenagers did not get on with him. To add to her problems, his business went into liquidation: 'At sixty plus, he had no chance of a job.' She had to go back to work. One day she was notified he had been rushed to hospital, critically ill. 'The children of his first marriage sat by his bed. I felt like an intruder.' When she left the hospital after the final visit: 'As a friend drove me home, I sat in the back of their car and thought, I'm a passenger again.' Not forever, it would seem, because she was introduced to another widower at a dinner party. 'We hit it off immediately.' Confronting her children with a decision to marry again, she met with apprehension from her daughter and amusement from her son. His first comment was, 'Here we go again.' Later, he was happy to amend this to, 'Mother picked a good one this time.'

Joan R. finally arrived from India to discover that she would not only have the responsibility of her three sons, but three stepsons wanted to live with her. The old friend who had offered to help was living in a small farmhouse in Kent which he had bought for his retirement. He had to buy a caravan as a makeshift dormitory for the boys. Building supplies were difficult to come by at that time, so there was no quick solution to the crowding. He gave up his bedroom to Joan and slept in the living room on the couch.

'The first time I knew James was fond of me was when I returned from a trip out in the night to the caravan to pot the children and found he had put an electric blanket in the bed.' Their courtship was more humorous than romantic. A little drive out in the moonlight found her in an exhausted sleep on her suitor's shoulder. She had come from a servant-filled life in India: 'twenty-six of them and one elephant' – to cook, clean and sew for a brood of boys. 'Your children need a father,' was how James worded his proposal. One must be filled with admiration for a man past sixty prepared to take on such obligations.

As soon as it was possible, he set about extending their home. 'He had already bought the farm and stables, but insisted on buying more land, then another farm, and suddenly we had 400 acres and 50 cows.' Guess who milked them? Joan had even more work on her hands, but loved every minute of it.

There have been similar happy endings for some of the ladies in other chapters. Cynthia finally recovered from the shock of Tom's suicide and began to go out again. A lot of men lost patience when her conversation centred on her late husband. Then she met one who was willing to humour her – for a while. But he asked her to stop talking about the past and pay some attention to her future – with him.

Frances Anne was bedevilled for years with nightmares about her husband, who was killed by a sniper. The dream followed her into a new marriage and two more children. 'Only then, I would dream my new husband was dead and wake up in a cold sweat clutching him and murmuring, "Thank goodness you're here".' This went on for a very long time. Then she dreamed he had run away with someone else. 'I woke him up to tell him what had happened. He said teasingly, "If you keep this up, that's what I'll do." He laughed me out of it and I never had those kind of dreams again.'

Her new marriage gave her something else: 'I had always wanted to be an actress. My husband said if I took a drama course, he would help me with the children – which he did.' Since graduating, she has had several successes on stage and film.

Jane sees many advantages to her second marriage. 'He is a younger man.' Her first had a tendency to irresponsibility, as well as concealing his age from her. 'This one is the better one, I don't have to think about bills. He is a proper responsible man.' She has also had another child.

Andra saw an immediate improvement in her children when a new man entered her life. 'They are much more settled'. As did Pamela: 'It did look for a while as though the world was full of married men. Then, at a family tea party, I was introduced to two bachelors. I married one. We have now celebrated our silver wedding.' This proves that there are several exceptions to the rule of caution when approaching a second time around. Children do need a father figure to turn to. Mothers who find him in a second husband are fortunate. Pamela rates as one of the best parts of her second marriage the fact that enough time has passed so that 'we can look back, share and smile over some of my son's escapades'. This not being able to 'share' a child's accomplishments or anything else he does comes hard to a widow.

Katie Boyle wrote an article on widowhood and a discussion she had with her late husband: 'I said, I would hate to marry again because you have spoilt me too much. I would always be comparing you to him. Poor man, he would have a terrible time.' Then, she met Peter Saunders. Their introduction 'sent a kind of electric shock through me and he seemed to feel it too'. A whirlwind romance followed and led to marriage.

The former Lady Melchett had said during her merry widowhood round of parties: 'I would never compromise where my emotions were concerned. I've always felt it was much better to live alone than make the kind of mistakes I've seen happen.' This lady was as entitled as any other to change her mind. Eleven years later, she met Andrew Sinclair and 'just knew, for the first time since I'd been living on my own, this was it.'

The luck would seem to be in the draw, first, second and even third time around.

11

Back to work or on with a career

'A new season to my life' – Mrs LBJ

'Over the years, you build up different things to do and make a new life for yourself'. Sooner or later, if a widow has any sense, she must accept that there is no alternative to following this advice.

Being committed in some way is the easiest path out. Certainly, the longer a career woman stays at home, the harder her loss is to bear. She has no experience of filling in house-bound hours. She knows nothing of domestic routine, which includes friends likely to drop in for a chat. Her professional world is usually separate from her home life. The quicker she gets back to work the better. This does not suggest she will function effectively at once.

As the book goes to press, Marina is still struggling. The book she was commissioned to write is unfinished. Her column goes on, but the strike picketing by printers at Wapping has made her life difficult. And now, there is no one to come home and 'tell my troubles to'.

Nevertheless, work does restore a pattern to the day. There is a part still which has not been damaged. A widow who has an occupation which holds responsibilities that have nothing to do with her husband's death is lucky. 'Going back to work as quickly as possible was better than thinking', said more than one.

A lady who had only taken a job at her husband's encouragement when their daughter died – 'I had become a "dressing-gown" lady refusing to go out and do anything or go anywhere' – now found that it was her rescue when she was widowed. 'Thank God, I had it to turn to.'

Having got herself back on stage, Barbara would later go into the award winning show, *Stepping Out.* Dorothy Lamour went on tour with a play: 'I work because I enjoy it and it has become therapy', she says.

Eleanor Roosevelt had resumed her column, 'My Day', the Monday after her husband was buried. She went on to personify 'keeping busy', with a magazine page, a radio show and, later, television. Her programme was to be the forerunner of chat shows. No one has topped her taking tea with Albert Einstein. At seventy-five, she was writing: 'When you cease to make contributions, you die.' She ended up being voted America's most admired woman, winning over Jackie Kennedy and Queen Elizabeth.

As wives, working women cannot afford to be too ambitious or their marriage may suffer. It is, after all, the rare husband who will tolerate his wife being continuously 'late at the office'. As a widow, she has no divided loyalties to stand in her way. Success, from now on, can provide a compensation. She can grow to love her career and find in it a fulfilment which is a substitute for a husband. Certainly something similar occurred for the woman who was a presidential assistant at the White House. 'The twenty-four-hour day demands of my job filled the emptiness of my life,' said Faith Ryan Whittlesey. She has since been promoted to be the US Ambassador to Switzerland.

Such women may have the first edge on those who stayed at home throughout their marriage, but circumstances can jolt Mrs Housewife into accomplishments of which she never believed herself capable. Many discover that they have learned much more than they thought in shop talk round the dinner table: 'I was a housewife who raised seven children. My husband died within 72 hours of a heart attack. That's how much time I had to prepare for taking over his company.' This lady admits she had absorbed a lot of company business 'by osmosis'. She made a great success of her undertaking.

If your husband's business is your only livelihood you have to jump straight in, as Hilda has discovered. Another woman quickly saw that 'the staff needed guidance – someone had to run things,' and she did it until she was finally able to sell this particular business as a going concern. It is all very satisfying especially if, in a marriage, a wife was constrained from criticism and interference: 'We didn't always agree, but I didn't want to interfere.' This is another proud lady who now runs the business her way – and successfully! Those who finally prove their point sadly find it is only to themselves, not to him.

Tiny Jennifer Castle in Florida was 'crewman' when her husband ran a school for seamanship there. She proceeded to earn a licence which enabled her to operate sea-going vessels up to one hundred tons and was appointed chairman and administrator in his place.

Many a board has learned to respect the business butterfly emerging from her domestic chrysalis. Helen is another example. Top executives expected to deal with the family business after her husband died. She felt she had the right to refuse them. She had been her husband's secretary before they married and knew how it all worked. 'Under my guidance, the company went from thirty million in the red to solvency. I'm feeling pretty good about the company and myself.'

This is no new phenomenon. In the eighteenth century Nichole Ponsardin, widowed at the age of twenty-seven, convinced her father-in-law that she was capable of taking over the Cliquot winery. She was so successful that her status was added to their champagne's name. Veuve Cliquot became big business, expanding into more and more vineyards. She did not even allow the Napoleonic wars to interfere with her progress; instead, she devised a way to get her sales agents through the battle lines. The greatest compliment to her endeavours must be the fact that champagne is affectionately known as 'the Widow'.

Sadly, years later, Moya Lear was not able to emulate Nichole. She tried hard to fulfil her husband's deathbed request: 'Make sure this company goes forward'. For a long time, she struggled to keep Learjet aloft, constantly changing its design and applying for the necessary certification. The plane ended up being nothing like the one he had designed, nor did it pass the necessary tests for the Federal Aviation Association. She had to stand by helplessly as the factory in Northern Ireland closed.

Stepping into a husband's shoes may not necessarily be to run a business. Joan Morecambe has been brought forward from the background where she kept herself as Eric's wife. 'How satisfying I should be asked to carry on his name in so many charitable organizations which he supported.' She spends a great deal of her time working to promote funds for charities like the Heart Foundation at Harefield Hospital and the Royal Society for the Protection of Birds, who propose to have an Eric Morecambe Memorial Bird Sanctuary in Essex.

After Congressman Hale Boggs disappeared in a plane crash in 1972, a special election voted his widow in to take his place. All the political lessons she had learned accompanying him on the campaign trail were to prove invaluable to her. She was eventually selected for the seat in her own right and is now on the powerful House Appropriations Committee: 'I don't think I would have been prepared for my current position if Hale hadn't helped me develop leadership qualities and the ability to recognize sources of aid and influence.' Lindy's new life has been built up from her husband's base, but it is now her own.

Other women may need to take a good look at what they have and see how they can use or adapt it to improve their lot. 'A full and varied life keeps me from falling into depressions,' says Jehan Sadat. She has not only become one of the most sought-after speakers on the US lecture circuit but is also a visiting lecturer on ancient Egyptian history at two American universities. There is still constant concern for her safety, so she never travels without bodyguards. A plane is sent to her American home to bring her to the campus. Classrooms and students are searched before she enters, but she does not let this inhibit the lessons.

The Middle East crisis some years ago brought the need for Arab countries to unify their efforts for aid and relief. They turned to Doctor El Said. She is now head of the Arab Women's Council. 'We started as a relief committee'. She devotes her life to improving the lot of others in this way and goes on lecture tours to many of the countries within the group. 'I have no bitterness of heart.'

Evelyn le Chêne is on the Foreign Affairs Commission of the European Union of Women and on the adoption list to be an MP either at Westminster or in Europe. She is still awaiting the trial of Klaus Barbie and has lodged complaint No. 80,326 against him: 'I shall be interested to look into the eyes of a man who could find it so easy to behave to human beings the way he did.' She feels some vengeance must be extracted on Pierre's behalf.

After Mary received her OBE she went into local politics. 'I started canvassing six weeks after my husband died and was actually elected to the Council within three months of his death.' Mary has found this a very satisfactory antidote to loneliness. She is not a woman who ever sits and stares at a silent telephone. Too many people in her ward have requests for her to check things like overhanging trees, defective drains, and all the other irritations that plague the local householder. 'In helping others, you help yourself.'

War widows in particular seem to feel strongly that they should do this. Several others listed the various groups for whom they raised funds. Many, from the Second World War, were women of a generation that were still raised to expect that 'gels got married'. The Battle of Britain pilot's widow had no training to turn to to support herself and what the children would need even though there was help for their education: 'I liked to work with my hands, so I took a course in millinery.' But at that time there was no future for hats. This 'gel' ran through a series of jobs, from barmaid to cosmetic adviser, as she struggled on: 'The Government have never faced up to the fact that our husbands gave their lives for King and Country, and should have shown their respect and gratitude for the supreme sacrifice by taking greater care of their widows and orphans.'

Marjorie, who had fought so hard for an allowance for her unborn child, decided: 'After the birth, I would put my baby in a nursery and carry on working. I couldn't do that. Sheila was such a great comfort I could hardly leave her a minute.' When her daughter was older, Marjorie trained to be a teacher and now feels she has had a 'full and interesting life'.

'Something old, something new.' This traditional requirement for a bride can carry over to the widow. Those who can, do reach back into a training like Marguerite Wolff with her piano-playing. They may have had a job that can be dusted off and used again – or given an extra shine.

In her single days, Jackie Kennedy Onassis had worked for a Washington newspaper. In her second widowhood, she decided to leave the world of fashion and frolics behind and go to work. In order to 'test the water', she first became a consultant editor for a publishing house. When her confidence was built up, she moved on to become a nine-to-five New Yorker with another one. Granted, she rarely struggled out of the subway or took lunch at a coffee shop counter, but she has blended with the City scene so successfully that when a policeman wrote her a traffic ticket, she had to spell her name for him.

Celia still has her voice. 'To be honest, I don't care very much about material things any more. I say to myself – why am I doing this? I don't have to, but then, I know darn well why I'm doing it. I'm not going to sit back and spend my days going out to lunch, tea and dinner. I am an achiever.' She began to record. 'Money brings boredom. If you don't have an occupation, you have nothing'. She began a whole new scene. 'I worked till I dropped'. The engineers at the studio asked her to stop, they were exhausted. 'I've never known such energy in my life'.

One of her albums was to have been called: 'Enjoy Yourself' but as she chose which songs to include, they touched too close to her emotions. 'Come in from the Rain' brought tears. 'He's out there in the cemetery' was her only thought. 'As long as he needs me' was as difficult to sing. In the end, the title was changed to: 'The London I love'. Since then she has produced and starred in a half hour video to display her talent.

Joan R. was to be widowed again in Kent. By then, her sons were at University. It is very satisfactory to record that they had clubbed together and bought her a string of pearls as a thank you for the contents of her jewel-box which she had used to educate them. She found the collection of farms too much to deal with on her own and sold them in favour of an hotel. Running it was not so simple as it first seemed. She had to give it up and bought herself a cottage. 'For a while, I knitted and played golf, but I got bored to death.' She took a college course in home economics – a rather amusing choice for a woman who had fed a full household with no training whatsoever.

Once qualified, she began as a teacher and was soon promoted to Head of Department, a position she kept until retirement fifteen years later. However, this was not to be the end of Joan's working life. She began to paint – well enough to sell several canvases. She also adapted episodes of her life for radio and lectures and is unlikely ever to run out of material. 'There are fourteen grandchildren, all inclined to arrive to visit me at once!'

The responsibility of being a sole parent may delay a return to a full-time occupation. Catherine, who is a doctor, devotes what spare time she has to a hospice for cancer patients. Louise, with a court case behind her, now knew her son's future was settled and he would be able to have the best of education. Now she could realize a dream: 'I wanted to make something positive out of something negative – my husband's death.' She enrolled in a drama school which resulted in some film, stage and television work after the course ended.

Anne, who felt 'I had been mother and wife for eight years, mother and widow for six' was now ready to extend her boundaries beyond voluntary work and make fuller use of her Bachelor of Science cum Laude degree. First, she became a consultant in special projects, for an oil company. Her job included the development and implementation of a series of special focus seminars. In addition, she managed the company's speakers' bureau. Her reputation for doing a good job must have spread. One day, the telephone rang. It was President Reagan calling from the White House to invite her to become the Cultural Attaché at the US Embassy in London: the first woman in history to hold that post.

Marie had always coveted a job in the hotel where her husband had worked as a musician. She is now hostess in the dining room there. She loves the fact that it is within sight of the piano Robert used to play. She looks forward to getting dressed up each evening to go to work: 'I have a social life without any obligations, except of course, to do a good job.'

That was exactly what Yasmine was trying to do. For a while she was thwarted by her accident. A relative helped her out with school fees until she recovered. Then she took a crash course in office skills, during which the students were expected to begin to apply for jobs. Yasmine was dismayed to find that she was turned down at every place she applied: 'They said I had no experience.' To voice a protest at what she saw as a ridiculous situation, she wrote to Mrs Thatcher: 'I asked her what sort of society she was creating when a woman willing to work hard could not get a job?' By way of reply, Mrs Thatcher arranged for an appointment for Yasmine with the Manpower Services Commission. However, in the interval between the letters, she had found something for herself. 'I wrote back to say, the society you have created is pretty fantastic – if you have the initiative, you can do it.'

The fact this job turned out to be boring made her decide to utilize a neglected law degree. It led to a position as a legal registration clerk. 'They said to set up their records would take two years and three people. I did it in six months.' She could have easily worked herself out of a job. Instead 'they gave me a beautiful office and asked me to stay on to maintain those records'. This was not a fulfilling enough occupation; she was looking for a greater challenge.

'I reasoned there must have been a great number of people like myself, suddenly left uninsured and vulnerable at the most difficult time of their lives. When you need it, boy, do you need it.' She applied to an insurance company for a job. 'They said with no previous experience in that field I was a lame duck.' They reckoned without her persistence! Yasmine convinced them at least to put her to the same kind of test as any other applicant. They wanted a little bit more from her: 'New recruits usually had to do twenty market surveys – I was told to complete seventy-five.' When she had accomplished that, they still put barriers in her way.

The minimum salary for a trainee was £500 a month. They offered her £400 and, in addition, 'when I was sent on the training course, everyone else was at an hotel. I had to commute to prove my cost-effectiveness.' One cannot be sure here why so many hurdles were placed to block Yasmine's path. It is an academic question, since she took them all with flying colours and came first on the course. 'By half a mark', she adds modestly. When one considers her daily three-hour journey back and forth while the other trainees were comfortably ensconced in that hotel to do their homework, her winning becomes more impressive. She was accepted. 'In the first month, I was on the company's production roll.' This was an honour that only she, of that course, won!

Yasmine does not present to clients as a conventional businesswoman. She has long flowing black hair and wears a sari. 'Chic, more than ornate for business, with simple jewellery.' This may be why, at first, no one was prepared to take her seriously. But she has proved otherwise. She has also evolved a put-down for the inevitable admirers. 'I tell them Muslims are against sex out of marriage and my motto is "No drinking, no smoking and no men."' Even more proudly, she will say: 'I'm a grandmother.' Few believe her.

Having conquered that frontier, Yasmine has other ideas in mind: 'This fantastic novel, that . . .'

Meanwhile Hilda struggles on with the business her husband wanted her to run. She is still beset by difficulties. Tiny of stature, it cannot be easy for her to 'boss' the workers, who, like the trees they minister to, are large men. 'Never mind, one day the sun will shine and my tummy will stop turning over each day with worry.'

She has the encouragement of all the other women in this chapter. If you want to make something happen, you can. Lack of education has nothing to do with not succeeding, if Joan R. is an example to follow. You just go out and get it.

12

Summing up

'You've changed'

Why do married friends expect that once a widow's grief has subsided, she will return to being the same person she was as a wife? 'It's altered my priorities and outlook on life. I no longer consider the same things important. Material things are all replaceable, John isn't.' This woman explains and echoes the thoughts of many. Still the accusations come: 'You've grown harder,' friends will say, oblivious of what has happened to make her that way. A combination of events adds up to the fact: it is the widow's lot, not the wife's, to have to write the last chapter of a husband's autobiography, as Bette Hill did. Nor can she come to terms with the fact: 'Graham survived 700 races, including 176 Grand Prix, to die in an air crash, when his approach to maintaining and flying his aircraft was more professional than professional pilots'.'

The thicker the skin the widow has to grow, the easier it turns to armour. She has to steel herself to smile at contemporaries still in pairs. While she may claim proudly: 'I've learned to travel by myself', mostly she would still prefer not to. Even harder to bear is watching those who are enjoying the pleasure of shared retirement – that luxury has been snatched from her. 'I still feel very angry. I wanted to do things with my husband and he's not here.'

So firmly have they been excluded from the life they had

before that they have every right to complain: 'Sometimes, you feel you hardly have the right to be a person, or even to live.' These bitter words, proved true so many times, make women begin to feel they are no better treated than the Red Indian widow who was put out of the tepee to exist only until she died.

A universal line of regret was: 'We were both too busy and now it's too late.' Conversely the fact that she is busier now is a form of rescue: 'It's so nice to come home and see the light blinking on my answering machine,' says Joan C. This is because her freelance work is expanding all the time, even to assignments abroad. She would still trade what a dinner-table party guest called 'such an exciting life' for what might have been seen as 'dull' evenings at home if she had her husband. These women may have adjusted to thinking for one, but it does not follow they will ever be really comfortable doing so.

There is no specific length of time before the pain eases. Each person's time-clock varies. While those bad dreams – 'I kept begging him not to die'; 'I kept dreaming he was coming back home and he'd find out I'd given all his clothes away' – will eventually fade, they may be replaced by something better. Those who are lucky will find they are the kind Mrs Graham Sutherland enjoys: 'The wonderful thing is I dream of him every night.'

Only the women who had endured unhappy marriages viewed widowhood with relief. Now they had a chance to get on with their own lives. But for most, the world will never be to their full liking again. The scars may not show, but they have been battered. Problems began for them from the moment of death, especially for the majority who had made no previous plans for this eventuality. Few couples make arrangements in advance.

Few women have training for the part of their married life which relates to death. They are rushed into decisions which they may regret later, be it the style of burial or the place of rest. While pressure from undertakers is not so great in Britain as in the USA, all undertakers are in business. They have the most vulnerable of customers. '"No" was my best friend,' says Lauren Bacall of how she managed to resist all the extras that were suggested as she prepared to bury Humphrey Bogart.

The greatest suffering was and is still endured by the women who never saw their husband dead. Without that evidence, they are left somehow unconvinced – and hopeful. 'I was sure it was all a mistake.' They go on looking for the man as if he had just disappeared – and could be found. 'In a crowd, you see the back of a head, a wave of a hand, and you think – that's him – he's not really dead.'

The manner, place and time of death can produce extra pressures. Victims of car crashes have great difficulty getting back into a car: 'Once I started physiotherapy at the hospital at Fort Oglethorpe, the nurse made me get into her car and took me for a drive round the grounds' – Pamela. While she got used to driving again she is still very anxious and afraid to travel on the date their accident occurred: 'I'm still not sure if I was supposed to have survived.' Another woman who got very panicky as the first anniversary of her widowhood approached found it was her turning-point – the stage at which she accepted what had happened.

What was apparent from most interviews was that those in authority need to correct many mistakes. 'The day my husband died, the tax man was at the door.' The British tax man who called on one widow was not that polite; 'He pushed his way in to calculate our assets.'

This unfeeling attitude extends in several directions. Those in authority should make sure they do not come single-handed with the bad news or offer it baldly. While having to pass on such bad news is no easy task for them, they have at least had more practice than the woman who receives it. They must know that she needs immediate support. Neither 'Come back later and see the body', nor 'Hurry and collect his clothes' is excusable. Nor is the situation where someone at a hospital forgets that an autopsy has to be carried out and the body is whisked back from the undertaker without notifying the widow: 'We went to the funeral home to finalize the arrangements and he wasn't there.'

Widows of suicide victims suffered the eternal question of 'Why?' One said: 'He robbed me of fifty years of memories.' Another: 'I would have coped better if he had died from cancer.' They are the ones at whom blame is pointed because, within living memory, attempted suicide in the United Kingdom was a criminal offence. Now, the successful ones leave their wives with the sentence.

War widows were the most bitter. This is understandable, when one considers their financial difficulties in keeping their children on a par with their contemporaries. One must wonder why funds contributed by the public tend to sit raising interest instead of helping to raise families as much as they might. One can, perhaps, understand that the sheer volume of casualties in the two World Wars precluded personalized help. 'Friends and relatives kept the baby supplied with clothes, plus gifts from America,' says Marjorie of how she managed. There was a significant war between that and the Falklands which left 'my children growing up with money so short, every so often I had to skip meals, sometimes it would be breakfast (I still wonder how I lived through those times). It was then I faced poverty in its truest sense.' At the very time this widow of the Korean war needed help (her husband had been declared missing – so she had to wait), it was not there. Mothers should not be forced to do without, or leave their children to go out to work, when funds which could support them have piled up.

One other striking factor about war was that each produced a widow who said: 'He left a healthy person and returned sick and never got better.'

Catherine, widow of the Falklands, takes a positive view: 'I'd rather have had five years with Chris, than not have had them at all.' Not that that furnishes her with complete compensation. When she is down, she says she takes her son to feed the ducks: 'I have to admit, they are getting pretty fat!'

Culture barriers, crossed as wives, can become insurmountable to widows. They may have to choose between their children and a new life. An American woman who married a Saudi nobleman now finds that she must relinquish her children to his family if she leaves the country. Other women who have departed from their homeland in marriage find that their children born on foreign soil adopt it as their own. They do not want to move back to what she sees as her home. She is left to choose between her homeland and her children and even her grandchildren who may also have arrived by then. Can renewing youthful memories overcome the possible loneliness she elects to choose?

The Orthodox Jewish woman has a different kind of choice if she enters into a new marriage. She no longer has the right to visit her late husband's grave. 'Loyalty is to the living.' This attitude may seem harsh but it does give a new marriage a better chance. Sikhs, Muslims and Buddhists have no such restrictions. Hindu widows have a problem, since within memory custom dictated that they burn on their husband's funeral pyre. They have yet to find a place within their society.

Widows of the famous – especially if their husband was a star – suffer the worst problems of rejection. Their social standing can disappear almost in mid-sentence at the funeral reception. It is interesting to conjecture how David Janssen's widow, so firmly dropped by all, later dealt with the deserters. She finally overcame her stigma by marrying a man of some power in the film world. Did she get her own back? One hopes so!

Some of these women will get the pleasure of acting as the star's surrogate voice from the grave. A silent star's widow made a profession of her role. Dressed in deepest black, Mrs Wallace Reid toured the country with her story. Peter Lawford's widow will do the same with a book. She has ample ammunition in his personal papers to fire shots across many bows. A friend reports: 'He told her everything about his life, so it should make interesting reading.'

Any relationship between a widow and a man seems to leave her wide open to criticism. The blame will always fall on the woman if anything goes wrong, as Elizabeth Taylor was to discover. Nor can Twiggy have a normal succession of boy-friends. Each one is branded as a potential husband. Widows of stars seem to do better if they remove themselves from the Hollywood scene. Shirlee Fonda finds New York preferable. Pilar, widow of John Wayne, moved down the California coast to Newport Beach and turned her talent for food into cook books and a restaurant. Maria Cole has retreated to Boston and involves herself in an anti-smoking campaign. (Nat King Cole, the singer, died of lung cancer.)

The greatest difficulty of a widow's life seems to be tied up in her being alone. The state of widowhood stays 'wrong' in people's eyes. Death has forced them out of the system of pairing which is such an integral part of social life. 'You are always the extra person at a party' – Lauren Bacall. She is backed up by one who remembers: 'Getting dressed up one evening to go to a party, looking in the mirror, being pleased with the result, then asking myself – why am I doing this – who for? – and I burst into tears.'

Katie Boyle, who had deliberately made herself too busy to think in the early days, said: 'Only several months after did I begin to realize how much loneliness, how much vulnerability, is welded into that word "widow".' To which Mary would add: 'There are far too many women who have left themselves helpless or dependent – they should have learned to drive.' In addition, those who cut themselves off at the beginning of their marriage by 'forsaking all others' have included female friends whom they now desperately need. Younger readers may find this strange, but their older contemporaries in widowhood were not very independent characters. A husband's interests came first and if he did not like their girlfriends, that was often the end of their friendship.

Widowhood seems to cheat a woman out of the ordinary friendship which can prevail between the sexes. It is a pity that the majority of men cannot understand that women may enjoy their company without any sexual intent: 'I often think many of them (men/other women's husbands) want to ease your frustration, and strangely enough they often think the way of achieving it is physical.' Are they very wrong? So much of what the widow misses is physical, if not necessarily sexual. 'It is the touch and smell of a man; the need to be hugged; the aggression of male conversation.'

But such attention does not seem to be able to stop at the point of conversation. Even a business woman finds this difficult to attain. However elevated the discussion, if she is known to be a widow, a leering wink hovers in the air. This leads to a woman having to downgrade herself to rebuff such overtures: 'I did it just once,' recalls Pamela. 'I admit I did half-suspect I would have to fend him off, so I dressed with deliberate care, making myself look my worst, not my best. It didn't make a jot of difference. If anything, the plainness I presented egged this man on – convinced him that anyone who had deteriorated as much as I, needed his favours as a restorative!'

Another was amused to discover: 'Because I was attractive, people assumed I was divorced. This included the men who asked me out. When I made it clear I was not a gay divorcee (in the old sense of the word) they were immediately more respectful. It did not stop them trying to take me to bed, it was just a less blatant overture.'

A growing number of such women see their singular situation as a challenge. Of course, a young widow left with small children has a long way to go before that happens. Having to endure the comments they receive from older women is bad enough. 'You're all right; you're still young.' Consider the responsibilities they have in raising children alone. Perhaps those constantly advocating single parenthood without really knowing what it means might like to reflect on sentiments repeated by many of the mothers who once had husbands to help raise their children: 'I cannot be two parents, and they need two.'

Widows left with children who are older, married or into their own lives and careers did seem better off. Even those who expressed disappointment in how they were treated had a subject of 'grumble' to offer in any conversation. Many have lost out because society no longer expects or is critical of unmarried daughters who do not stay home as a companion to 'pore ole widowed Mum'.

But the grown child's point of view should also be considered. They may have made a conscious decision to be cruel to be kind – and they must start their treatment as they mean to go on. The quicker 'mother' gets on her own two feet, they know the better she will be. What may seem heartless is true; if one is not pandered to, one has more to think about than self-pity. It may be painful for a while, but the majority of such widows will eventually see that this is the right approach. Such are the insecurities of this age that a mother could outlive any of her children, so she might as well learn to take care of herself.

It may have become obvious to readers that there are women in this book who have not yet arrived at the end of their Circle of Grief. Graham Sutherland's widow represents those who have chosen to live the life of a recluse. Before her husband died he made her promise not to do anything 'silly' (meaning, as she explains, an overdose). He also made her promise to live in an hotel where she would be cared for, which she does, but if he anticipated that that would mean she was surrounded by people, she is not. She keeps very much to herself.

What most widows lack is the feeling of being needed. They must do something to absorb the engulfing loneliness. No excuses must be accepted. There are plenty of charities that would welcome their help and quite a few unusual little jobs can be found. Those jobs that have what are termed 'antisocial' hours may well be just what the widow wants: 'Something to get me out of the house at a time I'd usually be preparing his supper.'

Even in a small town, there is something going on outside the front door. A glance through the local newspaper will show a plethora of coffee mornings, jumble sales, plus lectures and classes. Whichever way a widow goes, remember Sarah's advice: 'There is bound to be someone alone, longing for a smile which can lead to a conversation which can make a new friend.'

Before complaining that neighbours and friends keep their men from helping them, a widow must think back to her own married state. How did she feel about widows before becoming one herself? Did she enourage her husband to take care of 'that little widow next door'? One woman can now admit: 'All my life, I knew plenty of widows. I regret I wasn't kinder to them.'

It would be well to accept and not brood over what she sees as neglect from the friends of her married days. Most cannot understand how she feels. She must try to ignore the condescension of the wife who holds her husband up as a status symbol. The offensive comment: 'Never mind, you never know what's around the corner', which implies her man can easily be replaced. The impertinence of being asked: 'What do you do about sex?' from a complacent wife preening herself on her own husband's availability – to her.

Accept that such a woman will never understand until she is a widow herself. If it hurts too much, the answer is to find new friends. This is the main reason why widows end up seeking each other out. It's almost like having a special language that only they can share. If they want to repeat themselves they may, just so long as they return the compliment. Those who are not in this 'club' are apt to lose patience.

Because talking has been proved to be the best therapy, family and friends should allow a widow that release as soon as and as much as possible. If they do, the quicker will be her adjustment, and the less of their time will be required. However, that does not mean that once 'duty' is done, they should discard her. Remember, widows need to be tugged firmly, if not gently, into social contact. 'People had said, just come in, but somehow, I couldn't make the first move' – Joan C.

One must risk a widow bursting into tears and ask her round. After all, what is a box of paper tissues between friends? 'The greatest gift anyone can give you is Time, so if you can give Time to someone else it is a very special gift,' says Joanna.

Nevertheless, Sarah suggests the widow must try to put on a happy face for the public – to be a 'good value' guest. She stands more chance of being asked again.

What was most disturbing in researching for this book was to discover that widows do not seem to have won their independence in the eyes of the general public. Without a man, a widow is still seen as defenceless. There is an assumption from far too many people that she is not so bright as he was. Viv Nicholson, who coined the 'Spend, Spend, Spend' phrase after she and her husband had a fabulously large win on the football pools, found that all the bank accounts were closed to her when he was killed in a car crash. Trust funds had been arranged but the bank officials were totally unsympathetic to her needs and the fact she could no longer pay the children's school fees. But Alan Wicker, with whom she had made a television documentary, gave her some wise advice: 'Don't let them frighten you into moving. Get a solicitor.' Once the bank was informed that the will was to be contested, their arrogant attitude changed.

This illusion of helplessness is added to by the fact that the very people to whom the widow has to turn in the early days and weeks are men. This is inevitable while men are in the majority as doctors, solicitors, accountants, bank managers and garage owners. Is it their ego that keeps this picture of the 'helpless female' running?

These men, seen as father-figures/advisers and reliable shoulders to lean against, seem to be the very ones who are the doubters of the widow's ability. 'I think one of the most miserable things is this constantly being done down by others. I dare not go to a garage with my car before it is vetted by a friend.' There is a case here, when widows are contemplating embarking on 'something new', for taking a course in car maintenance or accounting. Talents such as these provide the sticks with which to beat back the patronizing attitudes they encounter and give them the confidence they need in their new single world.

13

Which way to turn?

A portion of the Jimmy Young radio show recently was devoted to 'Sorting out your Affairs'. This led to an unprecedented flow of requests for details of the leaflet on offer and indicated that for all the information that is currently available, many people have little idea as to what to do when someone dies.

Insurance companies have videos available on loan which show how to prevent some of the perils associated with widowhood. There are few takers from couples. One has to accept that 'when you die' is not a favourite topic of conversation between husband and wife or a subject for discussion round a dinner-party table, or a piece of evening's entertainment on tape.

It should be. Too few couples have even a cemetery in mind, let alone a burial plot bought. This lack adds even more stress to the widow's lot. It could so easily be avoided with a few prior words of discussion. In my own case, the untimely death of my husband brought a benefit to the majority of our friends. It made them realize that death does not only happen to the elderly, and jolted friends' husbands into explaining details of insurance and pensions to their wives, or wives into demanding to know what would happen to them if they became widows.

The DHSS publishes a booklet, D/49, which can be found in

places like the anteroom of the hospital office where one waits for the Certificate of Death. Hardly the time any but the most practical of widows would be likely to pick it up. Nor is everyone supported by a quick-thinking relative or friend at that time. The tact and helpfulness of staff in these circumstances varies with each hospital as does the follow-through to the widow at home. While most chaplains pride themselves on the fact there is a follow-up, it does not always happen. For all the good intentions, at this crucial moment a widow can be left floundering.

A good first stop, and one any widow should try to make, or be urged into making as soon as possible, is the Citizens Advice Bureau. Their claim, 'We are a door that opens to many', is borne out by several of the interviewees of the book, especially the one who did not know if her husband was alive or dead!

In more cases than is realized, especially under these circumstances, it is often easier to talk to a stranger than a friend or a member of the family. The wise widow will choose a time when there are not too many people around, like just after lunch. She is then more likely to receive undivided attention. But if the urge to seek help arrives on a busy day, she will still not be neglected. To the CAB, she is a person first, a widow second. This may be exactly the understanding that she needs right then – it is almost like shopping in a strange High Street, away from the people who 'know'.

Another early port of call should be CRUSE. It was founded for widows and named after the biblical story of the widow with the miraculous cruse of oil. The nearest branch will be known to the CAB or can be found in the telephone directory. At CRUSE, a widow can talk over her problems, which will be totally recognizable to those who listen. The immediacy of the help offered was amply demonstrated when I visited the head office. A lady came hesitantly through the front door. 'I'm newly widowed,' she managed to murmur. They gently ushered her into the privacy of a room where she could have a chat with a counsellor. They also operate a referral system.

One can be a good friend to a widow by contacting CRUSE for her. They will send a counsellor to her home, and if after a few visits she is still not ready to go out and meet other members, there is a monthly newsletter to which she can subscribe.

The Chronicle is a good introduction to the new world a widow must enter. Each issue contains encouraging articles dealing with different aspects of widowhood which continue to bedevil even the most well-adjusted woman. She will identify with members: they all share similar problems. The paper is like a family letter. All the writers are joined by the same tragedy. Friends made through this are more understanding of all things large and small. They know a leaky tap can be a crisis and how it feels when an electric bill threatens to decimate a bank account. No member can complain that there is 'nothing to do'. *The Chronicle* carries lists of classes, courses and retraining schemes.

Children also benefit. They come into a world where it is not a stigma to be fatherless, to be the odd one out at Sports Day at school. They share competitions, holidays and various other events where they are all alike.

There is also the National Association of Widows with its extension, the Widows' Advisory Service. This grew out of a pressure group with aspirations to secure improvements in widows' benefits and tax relief. As June Hemer, the founder, says: 'Widowhood is the single most common, personal catastrophe.' Officialdom never seems to recognize this. Therefore, the National Association of Widows has put out an excellent *Handbook for Widows* which is a clear guide to funeral, pension, wills and supplementary benefits. It offers suggestions on how the widow can afford to stay in her house, which she will probably not want to leave. There is also practical help on the security of the home and its maintenance, while pointing out the pitfalls attached to either do-it-yourself or so-called cheap labour.

However, it is usually too late by the time this handbook is brought to a widow's attention. The unexpectedness of widowhood is more the norm than long-range planning for death. At the time this book was begun Susan had no idea she would ever be included in it, she had a different kind of future ahead of her – or so she thought. Most husbands would be taken aback to find this book occupying an important place on the bookshelf. However, if a husband hasn't the courage to explain the finance of insurance, the house, or his pension rights to his wife before death, this handbook is a valuable asset to her recovery.

One of the greatest favours any friend or relative could do for a new widow is to obtain this handbook as quickly as possible and press it into her hand. Even if she is not yet prepared to accept the reality of her status, when she does, this seemingly 'cruel' act will be understood to have been kind. The fact that the *Handbook*, published in 1978, sold out its first printing within a month, proves how pressing is this need.

Bereavement Counselling Services are expanding their operations at a fast pace. Most libraries and health centres carry the local address. It may well be that in the early days it will need an understanding, helping hand to lead her there.

A widow should also be aware that she does not need to be on the brink of suicide to contact the Samaritans. They are there to listen to anyone who is overwhelmed with their life. They respond accordingly. Samaritans take the view: 'If they phone us, they want us.' Calls come in from widows most frequently on anniversaries and bad weekends. They reckon: 'Two or three calls and we've made a relationship. Then we would tell them what they really need. If they want to go to another organization, fine, if not, they can stay. So often, the people who come to us have been everywhere else. They are non-joiners. There aren't many places you can ring at 3 a.m. and have a chat.'

There is no need to telephone before going to the Samaritans' office. There are facilities there for someone who just wants to sit and talk – privacy, comfortable chairs. Samaritans can offer a 'befriender' – a particular person who will either be there when she calls or, if needed, visit.

Whether a widow has a religious faith or not, going to church is another means of communication with others. 'At least at the services, there is someone who will smile back. It is better than sitting at home all day alone. It breaks up my weekend,' explained one who is honest in the reason why she turned in that direction.

War widows are linked by the War Widows Association, but there is also the Royal Patriotic Fund for additional help. It would seem not everyone is aware of this. This is now an amalgamation of several funds set up to benefit widows and orphans of military men. All the donations they hand out, from spending money for a holiday, to financial assistance for the upkeep of a home or education for children, are meticulously recorded in an ancient ledger which dates back to Queen Victoria's foundation of the fund in 1854. Perhaps more war widows need to know about the extra facilities that can be there for them.

Mothers of young children also benefit from joining Gingerbread, originally formed by a mother in London who faced difficulties bringing up her children alone. While they cater for all kinds of single parent, they have plenty of help to offer the widow, including day nurseries which are a boon to those trying to hold down a job.

At the opposite end of life is Age Concern, which again has an interest in more than just the widow, but a great deal to offer her as well. If she feels she has not reached the age at which she needs their care, she might like to become a volunteer worker in the organization.

From a strictly social point of view, there are the old standbys: marriage bureaux. While many are computerized and unfeeling, plenty are not. They pride themselves on providing true friendship as well as marriage prospects. The ones that take the trouble to interview prospective members in their homes are a safer bet than those that just want a form filled in. But make sure they are not entering the house just to take an inventory of assets which extends to furniture and fittings!

Bridge players may well be able to stay put within the club of which they are already members. Those who want a 'new deal' may find closed doors. One woman solved this by taking lessons under the Adult Education scheme and thereby became invited into other groups known to the students.

There are also social clubs formed for the over-thirties which only ask for admission money to their various events. As they are not solely concerned with widows, they tend to limit their entry. Those investigated by the writer seem to supply something for everyone from lectures, concerts, coffee and cake mornings, cheese and wine evenings to dancing, nights out and group holidays.

An extension of the holiday idea which has no limitation to membership is Saga – if the widow is over sixty. Saga Holidays have been known to lead to more than one romance, though the organizers are quick to point out this is not the object of their exercise, just a pleasant bonus. They have a magazine which is full of informative articles and also includes columns of members looking for companionship. Anyone tempted by this should remember to stay behind a box number rather than offer an address.

The local YMCA is usually a hive of activity and if a widow is not looking for anything as physical as a keep fit class, as an onlooker she will still find the opportunity to make friends and indulge in some of the many other things that go on there. Take courage – take a chance – paste on a smile and GO.

As this book was written in the United Kingdom, it holds information primarily related to this country. However, certain other organizations have been brought to the writer's attention during research. There will be others, just a telephone directory away. All anyone has to do is LOOK.

The National Association of Widows has gone international and is linked with several countries, many of whom sent representatives to a conference held in the UK in 1985.

The Widowed Persons Service, Washington, DC, has programmes across the United States with a directory of branches.

Gold Star Wives is an organization of war widows in USA: they have a survival handbook for widows. Other organizations abroad include the War Widows Guild of Queensland, New South Wales and South Australia; Widows of South Africa; and the International Federation of Widows, Belgium.

The *Fédération Internationale des Associations de Veufs et de Veuves* in Holland has information for the widowed in all of Europe.

The International Social Service of Great Britain will help any reader wanting to assist a widowed person in another country.

The Mental Health Foundation, sponsored by National Westminster Bank Plc, brought out a self-help directory, *Someone to talk to*, in 1985 which is in the main branch of most libraries.

It is known that many towns in the USA have a Widow-to-Widow Counselling Service on twenty-four-hour call. Information about them will be found in the local Yellow Pages.

14

Tips on Survival

The majority of the following quotations have been left unidentified and will not necessarily relate to people met in the book as easily as the reader may think. For instance, would one visualize suggesting to someone who seems to be as busy as Kim Casali: 'You need to be needed – try and get an interest in helping in some way'? Sarah has a son who has been very supportive, but she still feels very strongly: 'You can't live on your children.' 'If you have children,' says another lady, 'try and think of them first and be thankful for them. Be mother and father to them but never make them feel they owe you. Don't tie them to your apron strings.'

Someone gave Lauren Bacall this wise piece of advice at her husband's funeral: 'Just know that every day, it gets the tiniest bit better – suddenly one day you can put it into a different perspective.' Katie Boyle has a theory that a widow 'must meet life halfway – resigning yourself to illness and boredom does nobody any good.'

It may be amusing for the reader to try to guess who said what in the rest. There are no prizes offered for the correct answers. The reward is to the reader, who will benefit from what she finds she can apply to herself.

What you must remember is, sooner or later, you have to

face reality. There is danger for those who try to make everything 'the same again'; 'Until I accepted this could never be, I could not recover myself.' The word zombie was mentioned by many interviewees. Pulling oneself out of that zombie-like state is the first priority.

Some of this advice may conflict. Some will appeal and hopefully spur you on. See them all as a Supermarket selection. YOU make the final choice on what you want to try.

Starting with the basics – the beginning – remember:

'We get out of life only what we are prepared to put into it. Accept the death immediately – one has to face facts.'

'Feeling sorry for yourself is destructive – being a whining, self-pitying person destroys everybody.'

'You need structure and discipline when you are alone, otherwise you tend to drift.'

'Life as a widow is, I suppose, an endurance test. Some days are better than others. The important thing is to get through each one.'

'The quicker you accept it is a new life the better.'

'You must develop your resources to the full and let perish any self-pity.'

'Keep off how miserable you are – how many stitches you had in an operation.'

'You must read the papers, keep up with what's going on.'

'Be occupied, not depressed – no one wants to know if you're in floods of tears.'

'Life is for the living – we cannot live with the dead.'

'Get off the idea that you need a man to survive.'

'Don't think because your husband has died, this is the end of your life.'

'Looking back, you get into a morass of self-pity – break into a new life.'

'Do as much as you can – Out. No good sitting on your bottom saying. "Poor Me".'

'Nor should you sit at home waiting for people to come to you – get out and help yourself.'

'You must have something to look forward to – go and find it.'

'Pick yourself up, dust yourself off and say, "Tomorrow is going to be better," it usually is.'

'Women should have passed a driving test and maintained their driving skills.'

If they haven't learned to drive here is something new to learn. There are far too many widows who have left themselves helpless or dependent on others by not being able to drive. It makes it all the more possible to follow the next piece of advice if one can drive.

'Do something every day, even if it is only meeting a friend for coffee or tea.'

'If I didn't get up each morning looking forward to something, I could easily become a basket case.'

'My motto has been – fill up every day.'

By doing so, you may do something for yourself and also help others. You can divert your energies to one of the several charitable schemes which would welcome your help. Never be put off by a first approach which may indicate an inviolate clique is in charge. Give them a second chance. If that is not satisfactory, look in the local paper. It is full of such information, especially what is going on at the local 'Y', as one widow discovered.

'There's something going on all the time, games and exercises, it doesn't cost much and there's someone to talk to. It's no good relying on your family.'

If you cannot find something you like, why not start an idea for yourself and anyone else who will join in? Widows' clubs such as they used to have in Valdosta, Georgia, USA, are probably a better bet at easing the widow into coming to terms with her singular life. They played cards, and took various trips. A similar sort of thing has been started in London by a widow who says there is a need 'to get together – begin a new social life'. This founder would like to see the success of her first group spread across the country. 'The great thing is to get people laughing – and they do.'

'Let yourself be happy, if you are happy. Don't feel obliged to be miserable all the time.'

'Be as independent as possible. You've got to be the sort of woman your husband would have wanted you to be.'

Unless, of course, he had hoped you'd pine away or had always said, 'You'll never make it on your own.' Now prove to him you can!

As has been shown, many women have another persona dying to get out. They will be happy to: 'Seek out a new road and walk down it.'

This does not necessitate a move. Far from it: 'When you become a widow, if possible, stay by yourself', or, put another way:

'Stay in a normal environment. If you move you're trying to run away from something, but you've got to take it with you all the time.'

'If you go and stay with someone you won't want to come home, and whatever you feel, eventually, you must.'

This applies to the very early days and how to cope with what at first appears to be an empty life. What to do later will be examined further on. What must come first is the practical side of life.

'Money for all necessities has to be sorted out first. This is irksome but builds a bit of a wall between the time of death and having to start living again.'

No one is advising that a door should be shut on a marriage, but it is a good idea to:

'Push the past into the background. Think about it – because you had wonderful years.'

'Start thinking about all the good things you have, not being sad about memories.'

'You must ask yourself what you are interested in and, as much as possible, pursue your interest. Your children will have more respect for you if you try to manage your own life, emotions and finances.'

Ill-health is no excuse, as a woman who has had nine major operations will testify:

'Whatever I have, I make it live with me – I refuse to live with it.' She leads a full social life which includes dancing, bowling and golf.

Someone else agrees with her:

'Resigning yourself to illness or boredom does nobody any good. Say "Yes" as much as you can to the outside world. You must meet life halfway.'

'Social life is very important – making new friends – keeping active – not expecting people to come to you.'

Not that you should not eventually repay those invitations!

'Invite your friends over as couples, have a dinner party for say, six, so men have company and the couples feel inclined to ask you back.'

When one widow began to entertain, she found a solution to seating which may suit others:

'I didn't want anyone sitting in my husband's place, so I bought a round table to replace the oval one.'

The question of a table setting leads to a warning from someone who went on a cruise because she felt it would be less lonely. It worked out well until she decided to take two days off on her own, on shore: 'The waiter showed me to a table for two but removed one set of plates and napkins.' This was repeated at every meal. It would seem even in the palatial surroundings of a five-star hotel they lacked this tiny drop of compassion. 'I sat in that great dining room alone. I could hardly wait for the ship to come back.' So, ladies, either don't get off the cruise ship for more than a tour when it makes port, or sit at a table for four, then someone is bound to talk to you.'

Not everyone can take a holiday unless they work. Work will keep one busy and occupied:

'Work is everything. If you don't have the education, go back to school, it can lead to a new career.'

'Make sure his death does not make you feel mentally as well as emotionally deserted.'

Some may be as lucky as Susan, and have a job offered to them:

'Never turn down any hand that's offering help. Never be too proud.'

But –

'Don't trust anyone until they prove their worth.'

'Be tough, don't undervalue yourself professionally.'

'Don't listen to people who tell you to stay home with the children – better to use earnings for help.'

This is a debatable point and one which may have to be reserved for those with children past the toddling stage. It is a personal fight between 'wanting to get out' and a duty to the child/children who are equally alone and should not feel deserted. Possibly you can turn to others: 'In-laws can be wonderful'. But that depends on their age as well as that of your children. Better yet, in this situation, to examine your skills: 'I began a little business making decorative cakes for all occasions.'

A new job can lead to a new life and, if you are so inclined, to better marriage possibilities, but remember:

'Few white knights ride down village streets looking for widowed maidens – you need to get out and meet them.'

What better way, than with a job?

Several suitable words of conclusion were offered.

'Drugs are no use, you have to face facts in the end.'

'Drugs would have to stop one day, then the hurt that had been tranquillized would all come back and I feel it would be worse than ever.'

This of course applies equally to those who have tried to wash away the misery with alcohol. Try not to let that sleep-inducing drink at night lead to too many others before morning. One lady said that the advice she had from a psychiatrist friend stood her in good stead:

'If you don't feel the need for counselling or tranquillizers, don't seek them' – and she did not, and managed.

To this must be added:

'Be strong, marshal your thoughts. I started to think "Oh dear", and then I thought: No, think back to how good it was, how lovely, how lucky to have had that.'

Which leads to a message from all the ladies who have been widowed to those who have not:

'Never take it for granted your husband knows you love him, tell him.'

Bibliography

BACALL, LAUREN, *By Myself* (Cape, 1979)
BARTON, WILLIAM E., *The Women Lincoln Loved* (Andrew Melrose Ltd, 1927)
BINGHAM, MADELEINE, *Earls and their Girls* (Hamish Hamilton, 1980)
Book of Facts (Readers Digest, 1985)
BRANDON, RUTH, *Dollar Princesses* (Weidenfeld, 1980)
BROWN, HARRY and PAMELA, *Those MGM Girls* (Harrap, 1984)
CHANDLER, CHARLOTTE, *The Ultimate Seduction* (Quartet Books, 1984)
COLLIER, PETER and HOROWITZ, DAVID, *The Kennedys* (Secker & Warburg, 1984)
DAVIS, JOHN H., *The Bouviers* (Farrar Straus & Giroux, 1969)
— *The Kennedy Clan* (Sidgwick & Jackson, 1985)
DU MAURIER, DAPHNE, *Rebecca Notebook and Other Memories* (Gollancz, 1981)
EDWARDS, ANNE, *Matriarch* (Hodder & Stoughton, 1984)
FURNASS, J. C., *The Americans* (Longman, 1970)
HEMINGWAY, MARY WELSH, *How It Was* (Weidenfeld & Nicolson, 1977)
HILL, BETTE, *The Other Side of the Hill* (Hutchinson, 1978)
HILL, GRAHAM, *Graham* (Hutchinson, 1979)
LASH, JOSEPH, *Eleanor and Franklin* (André Deutsch, 1972)
— *Eleanor: The Years Alone* (André Deutsch, 1973)
MCTAGGART, LYNNE, *Kathleen Kennedy* (Weidenfeld & Nicolson, 1984)
MANCHESTER, WILLIAM, *The Glory and the Dream* (Michael Joseph, 1974)
MASTERS, BRIAN, *Great Hostesses* (Constable, 1982)
NICHOLSON, VIVIAN and SMITH, STEPHEN, *Spend, Spend, Spend* (Cape, 1977)
PARKS, COLIN MURRAY, *Bereavement* (Tavistock, 1972)
SOAMES, MARY, *Clementine Churchill* (Cassell, 1979)